The
PAINTED
ROOM

The
PAINTED
ROOM

Ideas for creative
interior decoration

Kerry Skinner

David & Charles

A DAVID & CHARLES BOOK

First published in the UK in 1999

A catalogue record for this book is available from the
British Library

ISBN 0 7153 0840 8

Main photographs: David George
Step photographs: Tim France
Styling: Kerry Skinner and Tessa Evelegh
Designer: Robin Whitecross

Printed and bound in Great Britain by
Butler & Tanner Ltd, Frome and London
for David & Charles
Brunel House, Newton Abbot, Devon

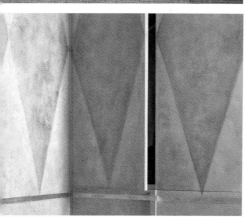

contents

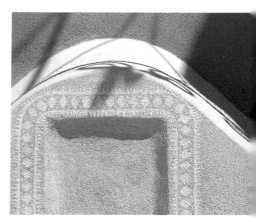

introduction

My purpose in writing this book was to bring together the various skills I have learnt, by trial and error, while striving to achieve effects which once existed only in my head or in that of a client with a daring and trusting nature. I have also tried to demystify the expanding market in materials and products for interior decoration, which can seem complicated and confusing to the beginner.

The first essential to bring to any project is enthusiasm. My own frustrated first attempts as a decorator made me well aware of the difficulties anyone can experience when limited by a lack of technical skills and training. Something that should be simple and quick - such as applying a colourwash - may prove time-consuming and difficult because the initial preparation has not been good enough, or you may lose heart when you find you have wasted money on products which don't live up to their promise. But with attention to detail and by following some simple rules, you can produce very satisfying results. Wonderful effects can be achieved at minimal cost if you spend some time doing a little research and experimenting with colours. The simplest techniques can convey the most complex of ideas, so I have always worked with the thought foremost in my mind that simple is best, tending only to add extra details and layers as I progress. Begin with thorough planning, with samples and ideas

This lustrous, sensual wall treatment was achieved with the simplest of materials and finished with light waxing to give subtle gleam: the technique is shown in detail on page 32.

boards and a clear idea of what you want to achieve, and you will be starting off on the right foot.

Colour is wonderfully expansive, and you could spend a lifetime trying out all the various combinations, before even beginning to deal with structural, textural and figurative elements. It has been said that colour is the natural voice of the subconscious; an understanding of our own intuitive response to colour can give us all an awareness and responsibility for our own happiness and sense of well-being. It is natural to choose colours which stimulate, soothe or enhance our enjoyment of life and work, but often the dictates of fashion can distract us from our personal vision. Confidence is the key and through interesting projects, learning the logic of colour theory and breaking the boundaries of preconceived notions is easy and fun.

To simplify a project, and to eliminate the margin for error, remember that less is more and stick to multi-purpose materials and equipment that can be easily obtained. I enjoy the variety of effects I can achieve with a sponge, for example: an everyday object, it has been the tool for realizing many sophisticated and original techniques. My personal interest has always been to achieve a variety of decorative effects with as little environmental impact as possible, and biodegradable materials and minimum waste are important considerations when

Textured paint and clever colourwashing have transformed a plain wooden fire surround, now convincingly disguised as elegant dressed sandstone (see page 62).

planning a project. Manufacturers are usually happy to discuss these concerns and, noticeably, have begun to offer more choice for the discerning decorator.

This book does not contain templates because it is not necessary to copy anything - all the motifs used are very simple and serve as devices to introduce an element of colour. The square is used on a number of occasions as I love the balance and regularity of the shape; combining it in different scales and with different colours can be very satisfying. Geometric forms offer a range of straightforward shapes for adding colour and decoration in sympathy with their surroundings. Conceptually balanced and rhythmical, they combine simplicity with a timeless quality and appeal.

It is both my belief and my experience that everyone has their own, unique creative potential. I have absolute faith that given basic guidelines, it is within us all to produce something beautiful and life-enhancing. A focus of intent, and being happy and relaxed while working, are crucial. Above all, remember that most mistakes can be rectified very easily and putting them right, though humbling, can be the beginning of a new journey of self-expression. It is my hope that this book will inspire you to take up the challenge and enjoy creating interesting and inspiring projects of your own. Use this collection of ideas as a starting point, to be interpreted as a helping hand rather than a prescribed method: it will soon become clear that practically every surface can be decorated with colour and that the techniques shown on the following pages are open to endless - and personal - variation.

understanding colour

As an element of form, colour has stronger influence, can arouse greater appreciation and will stimulate more thoughts and feelings than any other visual aspect. It can be used as a device to create a comfortable or exciting ambience and to influence mood. You may be able to work with colour instinctively, but if you understand its use you will feel confident and be able to experiment with it more successfully. The use of colour is a skill which needs to be learnt like any other. A study of the colour wheel – its potential, values and the relationships between colours and colour combinations – is essential.

The colour wheel

Contemporary colour theory is based on the spectrum: that is, the colours seen when white light passes through a prism. A rainbow is the manifestation of sunlight passing through raindrops but in reality its colours are more diffused than the manufactured version we use as reference: this is known as a colour wheel and is invaluable in learning about colour. It consists of bands of red, orange, yellow, green, blue and violet arranged like the spokes of a wheel to show the colours in relation to each other more effectively. The three primary colours, red, yellow and blue, create the secondary colours – green, orange and violet – when two of them are mixed. Mixing equal parts of primary and adjacent secondary colours produces tertiary colours. For example, red and violet make crimson, blue and green create turquoise and yellow and green create lime.

The qualities of colour

A particular colour can be defined by referring to its three qualities: **hue, value and intensity.**

Hue is the specific spectral name of a colour, such as red, blue or green. It differs from 'colour': the colour pink, for instance, is a red hue.

Value refers to the darkness or lightness of the colour, and encompasses tints, shades and tones. Tints are created by adding white to the colour, shades by adding black. You can get a clear idea of tones by looking at the colour wheel: it is easy to see that yellow has the brightest tone and violet the darkest, with red and green appearing as similar, often the same.

Intensity refers to the saturation of colour: its purity, brightness or dullness. When a colour has a high intensity it is bright, strong and clean, as opposed to muted, dirty and dull.

Describing colour

Once you begin to use colours in a practical way, you need to consider not only their individual qualities but also the effects they have on each other. The mood you create when decorating a room will depend to a great extent on the range of your palette.

Monochromatic A composition of several values or intensities of a single colour involves a range of tonal sequences of the colour. This can be achieved by adding neutrals such as white, grey and black, or small amounts of the complementary colour. It can also be based upon the neutrals alone, with combinations of taupe, beige, sand, cream, grey and white. The introduction of varied textures can create more interest in a neutral scheme.

Analogous (adjacent) Calm and restful schemes can be devised using adjacent hues on the colour wheel, combinations of which appear harmonious as the eye travels easily between them.

Complementary (opposite) Complementary colours are diametrically opposed on the colour wheel. Examples include red and green, blue and orange, and crimson and lime green. These can create stimulating mixes with a lively impact. Introducing small amounts of a contrasting colour to the uniformity of a one-colour scheme is a simple means of achieving balance and resolution.

Contrasting This can be a striking combination of neutrals such as black and

white, black and yellow or blue and white, or might use the clashing primaries against white that can be seen in the paintings of Mondrian.

The quality of warmth or coolness of a colour can have an impact on our emotions in response to it. Red suggests passion, action and danger; orange vibrancy and health; and yellow happiness, warmth and sunshine. In contrast, blues can suggest space, coolness, tranquillity and melancholy. The placement and quantity of colours can create the suggestion of colour advancing and receding; bright, warm colours tend to advance while dull, cold colours recede.

Our emotional response to different colours is closely linked to their environmental associations. For example, green suggests growth: it is refreshing, cooling, assisting renewal. Brown suggests earthiness, harmony and humility. Purple is the finite colour combining warm and cold, distant and near; it is often viewed as inspirational, spiritual, religious and soothing.

top: A painting in soft, muted tones of yellow ochre, siennas and blue, set against an ochre colourwashed wall on a gold shelf, becomes part of the space, merging and blending with its background.

middle: The blues in this painting tend to recede, but they stand out in contrast to the warmer background colour on the wall. The contrast has the effect of making the yellow of the wall more pronounced.

bottom: The red painting brings out the warmth of the yellow wall, but also sets up a vibration with it as the red is a stronger, deeper tone.

decorating with colour

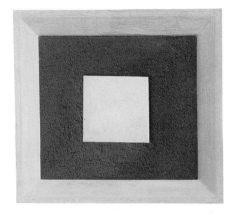

In this aquarian age, decorating has taken a new turn. Contemporary schemes rely on natural colours: greens, browns, taupes and off-whites, elevated by lilac, mauve and plum. The use of softer, more sensual, natural materials predominates. This is balanced by the use of simpler outlines in the shapes of furniture and accessories. Decoration appears less as an expression of material wealth or status, and more as a visual manifestation of a need for harmony, relaxation and a sense of oneness between the natural world and the built environment.

Everyone has a personal combination of colours they like to look at and wear. This subjective selection and use of combinations of colour not only makes different environments individually attractive but should also be seen as a process of self-discovery. The use of colour and, to a lesser degree, pattern and texture can elicit strong responses.

left: Close one eye and stare at the grey squares at the centre of each sample. The grey area will soon become imbued with complementary colours as the eye can't cope with too much of one colour.

right: top row, left to right lilac colourwash behind terracotta crackle-glaze with rubbed-in gold; sponged, stippled pale green behind umber plaster effect; soft lilac colourwash behind dark green and blue crackle-glaze

2nd row, left to right terracotta and white crackle-glaze behind deep copper metallic; orange colourwash behind verdigris crackle-glaze; plnk stucco behind cobalt blue colourwash

3rd row, left to right blue colourwash behind green, white and taupe crackle-glaze; lilac stucco behind red colourwash; black and gold marbling behind yellow ochre colourwash

bottom row, left to right yellow plaster effect behind ultramarine plaster effect; pink/lilac colourwash behind lapis lazuli effect; pink/brown crackle texture behind gold

Colours and textures

The texture and nature of the surfaces to which you apply colour will have a marked effect on how it is viewed. A matt or rough surface will appear darker than a shiny, glossy one due to the difference in reflected light. Apart from aesthetic, subjective reasons for your choice it is worth considering the surface texture chosen in terms of its practical suitability. Smooth surfaces are more appropriate for use in areas which need cleaning often, such as a kitchen, whereas a coarse, more textured wall surface might be best used in an area where you want to suggest softness, intimacy and casual comfort, as in a sitting room or bedroom.

It is very important to consider the quality and intensity of the light available, and as daylight and artificial light behave very differently, it is always best to view samples in a variety of lighting. Halogen bulbs issue a whiter light than ordinary household bulbs, while natural light varies with the seasons and all light is affected by the choice of curtains and lampshades.

Metal, glass and mirrors can all be used to reflect and diffuse colours and light. The balance of light, colours, tones and textures must be considered carefully in each area at the start of any project.

Paint

Paint could be considered every decorator's best friend as it is the easiest way to introduce colour to a scheme. It is also the cheapest and quickest method of transforming a room, and if you have a new idea it can be changed yet again,

literally at the stroke of a brush.

Paint contains two main ingredients: colour in the form of pigment, and the medium that carries the colour. Previously, paint used either water or oil to carry pigment but modern production methods allow a blend of synthetic resins and plastics to be used. Although they make paints that are tough and easy to use, the disadvantage of these binders is that they encourage an overuse of non-renewable resources and create a product which is less environmentally friendly because the ingredients do not break down easily. It is to be hoped that a return to the production of more traditional paints will ensue, and already organic pigments, binders and solvents are becoming more readily available. As the processes of decorative painting become demystified, traditional techniques such as limewashing, distemper, colourwashing and simple plastering are becoming more widely used once again.

samples and ideas boards

When deciding on a colour scheme or a theme for your decoration, it is easier to begin with some reference point. This could be a favourite object, colour, fabric swatch, or image such as a painting, postcard or photograph. This will help refine influences and rationalize the scale, and should make the overall project seem less daunting.

The best way to collate the various pieces of inspirational information you are using is in the form of an ideas board (you can use a large sheet of paper). It is important to keep samples in proportion: for example, if the wall finish or flooring is to be the backdrop to other smaller decorative devices, try to have this as the largest sample and set the others against it. Use a variety of scales of decoration and pattern – photocopying can help enormously with this.

Take time to assess separate boards against each other and in different lights. They will help you to clarify your aims and intentions. Experiments with the density of mixes and colours, with combinations of ideas, colours and textures are all homework which can be fun and exciting.

You may find it useful to compile, as work in progress, a general chart of your favourite colour combinations: draw ideas from the effects achieved by others, and keep notes of what you liked about them.

Before beginning any decorating project it is always useful to prepare a piece of board or lining paper with the same base colour and texture as the actual surface and experiment with paint in washes, textures and depths of colour. This will give you more confidence as you learn how different paints will behave, and should also mean that when it comes to the real thing the work can be more spontaneous and relaxed.

The colours used in this book tend towards a palette of earth colours with fresher, brighter splashes. These more tropical colours are rarely primaries but are usually secondary colours softened with white. Texture is very important in the realization of colour, with pattern kept to a minimum. Where pattern appears it is usually simple, using naive, geometric shapes, and is often just a device to introduce colour.

wonderful walls

stucco plaster effect

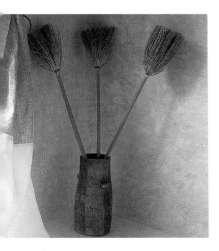

In the kitchen of a large airy town house, used frequently for entertaining, the walls are suffused with a warm, cosy glow. To achieve this inviting look, stucco has been mixed with burnt sienna pigment: the result is the warm terracotta colour of fresh plaster, yet the walls are imbued with a sensuous softness by the sheen of the polished stucco. The glow and warmth of reflected light, diffused through unbleached linen curtains, gives the room a welcoming atmosphere during the day as well as in the evening. The earthy feel of the terracotta walls is emphasized by the natural softening of the corners and edges of walls and shelves caused by the layers of plaster. This warm pink finish acts as a wonderful background to a display of rustic and organically shaped pots and bowls. It is an uplifting, flattering colour to live with, working well with a mix of mellow wood tones and sharper, brighter colours and metallics.

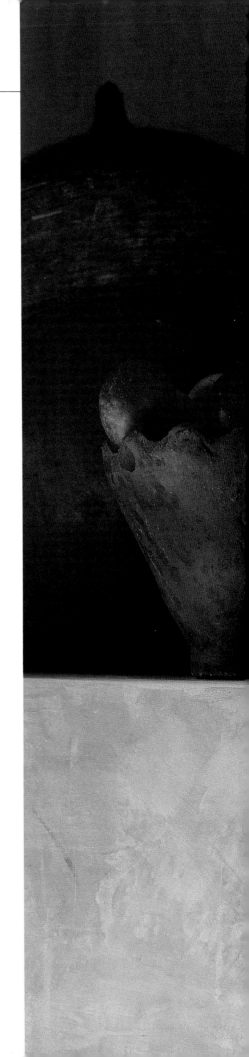

The deep fitted shelf is given the same warm, decorative finish as the walls to tie it into the background.

Focus on Technique

Stucco has a harder finish than ordinary plaster yet is quick and easy to repair as long as samples of colour and mixing ratios for the pigment are recorded when it is first used.

Materials and Equipment

matt emulsion in rose white
paint roller and tray
paintbrushes
plaster sealant
pigment for colouring plaster
mixing container
white stucco plaster
sealed board for mixing plaster
plasterer's steel float and hawk
gloves and cloths
medium wet-and-dry sandpaper
filling knife
sponge (optional)

Preparation

All the walls and built-in floating shelves are painted in rose white matt emulsion, applied with a roller.

1 Prepare the painted surface for the stucco plaster with a thin glaze of plaster sealant. Work it in well using a paintbrush and leave to dry.

4 To apply the next layers use a steel filling knife. To bevel the edges of the blade, dampen some medium grade wet-and-dry sandpaper and lay it on a flat surface. Hold the blade at a shallow angle and rub the edge in a circular motion. Smooth off the corners.

5 Carry a small amount of plaster on the steel float, leaving the rest under a damp cloth as it will dry out quickly. Apply the plaster in a series of thin layers, beginning at the edges of the walls. Use a sponge or a gloved finger to smooth it carefully in the corners.

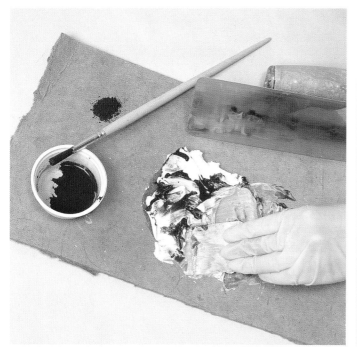

2 Carefully follow the manufacturer's instructions for adding colorant to stucco, as variations occur. Dilute the colorant in water and add to the white stucco plaster. Mix only small amounts at a time and check the colour constantly against a sample area to achieve consistency.

3 Using a plasterer's steel float and hawk, apply the first coat to the wall. Pull the plaster thinly and evenly across the surface. Always wear gloves when working with plaster.

6 To cover a large area use a continuous motion, pulling and wiping thin layers with regular movements, changing direction often. The blade will need to be cleaned regularly with a damp cloth and occasionally re-bevelled on the sandpaper.

7 When the plaster has dried it can be buffed up using a clean blade and a soft cloth.

découpage wall

This individual alternative to traditional wallpapering will hide cracks, bumps and uneven surfaces. It is quick and easy to apply once you have assembled a collection of papers, which can range from cheap and cheerful recycled materials to beautiful handmade paper with interesting and unusual textures. Used in this way, a few sheets of exquisite plant and tissue papers can make a huge impact in a large-scale decoration. The papers and colours you select can echo the fabrics and furnishings in the room: if you want to accentuate a particular colour, it is a simple matter to paint some of the paper before you add it to the design. The elements of the pattern can be as large or small as you wish, adding ornamentation and beautiful textures to the decorative scheme. In this room, the other walls are painted ochre and the collage introduces highlights and accents in the same colour range, such as gold, cream and brown, as well as balancing the warm tones with soft blue-greys and sparkling white.

This multi-layered collage is easy to change, or to paint over, and makes an interesting project for everyone in the family to participate in. The decoration is simple to do, yet has an impact like a painted or printed pattern on canvas or fabric.

Use painted and textured papers in a découpage wall treatment to create a focus of interest on a prominent wall such as a chimney breast.

Focus on Technique

This simple technique uses paper to cover a wall. The finished effect is ideal for uneven walls that may have needed too much filling to achieve a finish suitable for finer effects.

Materials and Equipment

matt emulsion in orchid white
paint roller and tray
paintbrushes, artist's and varnishing brushes
tape measure
pencil and steel rule
handmade tissue and thin textured papers
 in neutral colours
artist's acrylic paints: gold and yellow ochre
paint kettles
PVA glue
decorator's sponge
dead flat oil-based varnish
white spirit

Preparation

The wall is given two coats of orchid white matt emulsion, applied with a roller.

1 Measure the wall to work out how many 14cm/5in squares will fit vertically and horizontally. A border can be created down each side if you want a framing effect. Starting in the centre of the wall, mark out the grid with a pencil and ruler.

4 To apply the découpage, mix one part PVA glue with two parts water. Lay the squares out on a clean flat surface and glue on the various patterns, using a brush to smooth the paper down.

5 To apply the squares to the wall, paint the wall with glue, then position each paper square carefully and smooth down with the glue brush. Fill in all the squares and add decorative details until you are happy with the design.

2 Select a variety of different papers and mark out the required number of squares. Tear the squares using a steel rule, to give the paper a soft edge. Prepare some of the squares by painting them with washes of gold and yellow ochre.

3 Most of the paper squares are decorated with découpage patterns. Using a ruler, tear strips, squares, crosses and lines as you work out the designs for each square. Leave some squares plain to avoid making the pattern too busy.

6 Leave the glue to dry, then sponge on a thin wash of ochre acrylic paint in places. Allow to dry.

7 Finish the wall with a dead flat oil-based varnish diluted 2:1 with white spirit. Brush it in well to prevent runs.

lilac crackle-glaze panelling

Soft lilac white crackle-glaze has been chosen to give a subtle texture to imitation tongue-and-groove panelling in a bathroom. A splashback has been created around the bath using MDF panels routed to resemble traditional tongue-and-groove, and a finish that resembles weathered, painted wood, adding tactile as well as visual interest, enhances the illusion of real planking. With its echoes of sun-bleached panelling on seaside structures, the finish has an affinity with its watery setting.

As this panelling is functional as well as decorative, it needs a hard-wearing, easy-to-clean surface. The use of eggshell and matt emulsion strengthened by the addition of filler gives the finish a durability suitable for this situation, and two coats of tough, oil-based varnish help to keep the paint effect stain-resistant.

The freshness of the delicate colouring balances the deeper tones of the warm blue shallow shelf above the panelling, and the more vibrant lilac colourwash on the walls.

Crackle-glazed in two shades of soft, pale blue, wood panelling makes an atmospheric splashback around the bath in a lilac bathroom.

Focus on Technique

The crackled paint effect finish is easy to do and very hard-wearing. Adding filler to the emulsion paint gives it weight which means the brush strokes need to be short and quick, with little over-brushing. The extra protection of varnish is only needed where the surface will be prone to constant splashing.

Materials and Equipment

oil-based eggshell in warm blue
paintbrush
all-purpose filler
mixing container
dessertspoon
paint kettle
matt emulsion in blue white
hairdryer or hot air gun
fine wet-and-dry sandpaper
cloth
matt or dead flat oil-based varnish
flat varnishing brush

Preparation

The imitation tongue-and-groove panelling is prepared with acrylic primer and tinted oil-based undercoat.

3

To assist the drying process and to ensure the crackle-glaze works as evenly as possible, use a hairdryer or hot air gun to warm the paint. Do not hold the heat source too close to the surface as this may cause blistering. Move the heat constantly over the surface, working from a distance of at least 60cm/2ft.

1

Paint the surface, including the shelf above the panelling, with two coats of warm blue eggshell. Allow the first coat to dry completely before applying the second. Apply the paint as evenly as possible, ending with a downward brushstroke each time.

4

Leave the crackle-glaze to dry thoroughly for at least 4 hours, then sand it lightly with fine wet-and-dry sandpaper to remove any roughness from the surface. Wipe off the dust with a brush and damp cloth.

2

While the second coat is still tacky, apply the top layer of paler blue. This is a mix of matt emulsion and all-purpose filler. To prepare it, follow the manufacturer's instructions for making up the filler, then add about 40ml/4 dsp to each 0.5 litre/ 17 fl oz of paint. Mix this well until it has the consistency of double cream.

5

To protect the paint surface against water damage, apply a matt or dead flat oil-based varnish. The varnish should be applied with a flat brush, ending with a downward brush stroke each time. Apply two coats of varnish and leave to dry thoroughly.

burnished gold wall

Painting a wall entirely in gold gives an illusion of depth and solidity. It also takes on a fabulous elegance and makes a perfect background to a display of treasured paintings or special objects. A painted gold surface is less reflective than real gilding, but it has a soft glow which is unique. On a large area where gilding would be oppressive, light soft gold paint looks atmospheric and sophisticated. The chequered effect is easy to achieve, and adds interest to what would otherwise be too uniform a finish on a large expanse of wall. When waxed, the finish has a sensual vibrancy which it is not often possible to achieve with cooler colours, and it feels as good as it looks – rich, smooth and plush.

The wall is broken by a shallow shelf which has been decorated with the same paint effect. The surrounding walls are colourwashed in ochre, a colour close in tone to the gold paint, so that it appears in harmony with the rest of the decoration, rather than standing out in garish contrast. The finished effect is subtle and quietly opulent.

Touches of gold in the rest of the room, on objects and decorative details, ensure that the gold-painted chimney breast harmonizes with its setting.

Focus on Technique

The chequered effect is achieved quite simply by painting through a square stencil and alternating vertical and horizontal brush strokes. The deep red undercoat helps to enrich the colour of the gold.

Materials and Equipment

matt emulsion paint: white and deep red

paint roller and tray

paintbrushes

fine sandpaper

tape measure, pencil and ruler

stencil card

craft knife and cutting mat

lemon gold powder

paint kettle

PVA glue

masking tape

wax polish and soft cloths

Preparation

The wall is painted with white matt emulsion, then rubbed down lightly with fine sandpaper.

1 Brush on two coats of deep red matt emulsion paint. The brush strokes should be varied in direction to ensure an even coverage. Lightly sand with fine paper.

4 When you reach the edge or the bottom of the wall, cut the end off the stencil or have a stencil cut ready to fit the space available. Paint these part-squares with vertical strokes as before.

2 Measure the area to be painted and mark up with evenly spaced squares in a grid, starting in the centre of the wall; this will be the guide for positioning the stencil.

3 Draw and cut several square stencils to fit the grid. Mix two parts gold powder, one part PVA glue and two parts water. Fix the stencil in place with tape and steady it with your spare hand. Paint alternate gold squares starting at the top of the wall and brushing the paint vertically in a series of short, quick strokes.

5 Fill in the remaining squares with the gold brushed through the stencil in a horizontal direction.

6 When the wall is dry, protect it with a layer of wax. Apply it with a cloth, then polish off and buff the surface to a soft sheen.

lilac colourwash

The colourwash for this bathroom has been built up in layers of reddish pink and warm blue which combine to create a restful lilac shade. The shelves, cupboards and walls have all been given the same treatment. The colour was chosen to create a romantic, relaxing environment that would help to soothe away the worries of the day. Linen gauze curtains soften the light from the window to ensure a restful atmosphere during the day.

This wonderful realization of balanced warm and cool shades of colour suggests calm and ease in the bathroom. Lilac has long been viewed as a calming and harmonious colour, associated with religion and spiritual ease. The finished surface has a chalky quality, which enhances the gentle ambience of the room.

The stencilled wave decoration suggests the theme of water, and draws attention to the narrow shelf which circles the walls around the bathroom for the dual purpose of storage and display.

The soft mixture of pink and blue on the walls means that furniture and accessories in either colour fit equally well into the scheme.

Focus on Technique

The end result of two-colour layering is a lilac paint effect that looks delicate and ephemeral but is in fact very durable. Painting the shelves and cupboards with the same washes gives a very restful and soothing atmosphere to the whole room.

Materials and Equipment

matt emulsion paint: rose white, warm blue and pink
paint roller and tray
masking tape
paint kettles
decorator's sponge
small and broad paintbrushes
matt emulsion glaze
pencil
stencil card
craft knife and cutting mat
small foam paint roller head

Preparation

The walls and shelves are rollered in rose white matt emulsion paint. Any meeting points with other paintwork should be masked with tape.

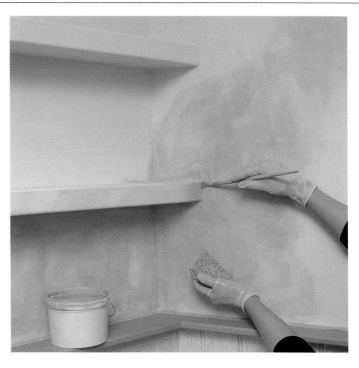

1 Dilute the paint for the colourwashes 1:2 with water. Apply the first layer of warm blue using a sponge. Use a small brush for the corners and edges.

2 When the blue has dried, apply the pink wash in the same way, sponging over the whole surface as before. The wall colour should begin to appear to change to lilac, but still needs to be built up. Alternate the coloured layers until you have achieved the required density, and leave to dry.

3 Apply a softening coat of the base colour diluted 1:2 with water. This layer should be applied in a more patchy way, allowing areas underneath to show through. As this is a bathroom wall, protect it with a thin coat or two of glaze, working downwards in a zig-zag way.

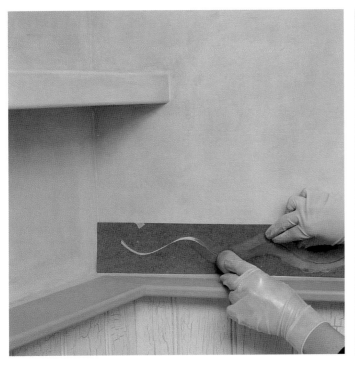

4 Draw and cut the wave stencil, attach the card to the wall with masking tape, and apply metallic blue acrylic paint using a foam roller head. This leaves a regular, even stippling in a very thin layer.

5 The curl of the wave is stencilled separately, and should be applied carefully to fit the end of the wavy line, angling the curl to suit the meeting point.

floors and floor coverings

limed effect floor

Stripped or sanded pine boards make a satisfying and sympathetic flooring – smooth, even and comfortable to walk on – but when sealed with varnish they usually take on an unattractive strong yellow appearance. A lime-washed effect can also be used to knock out the bright yellow of new pine: it suggests a bleached look, but adds a protective layer to the floor, giving the wood a completely smooth, strong finish without sacrificing its texture or obscuring the natural variations of the grain.

Liming, which this technique imitates, is a traditional treatment for oak panelling. It entails opening up the grain of the wood and filling it with a dense white paste of unslaked lime, before applying a finish such as French polish. The overall effect is subdued, but fresh and clean. A lime-washed floor provides a neutral background to any decorative scheme, preserving the pale, light-reflecting quality of new wood while eliminating its brashness. The soft, natural-looking finish is sympathetic to any other textures and colours used in the room, fitting in as well with bright colours and modern furniture as it does with subtle earth tones and natural materials. The floor offers a quiet, smooth surface to adorn with rugs and mats; it is pleasant to walk on and easy on the eye.

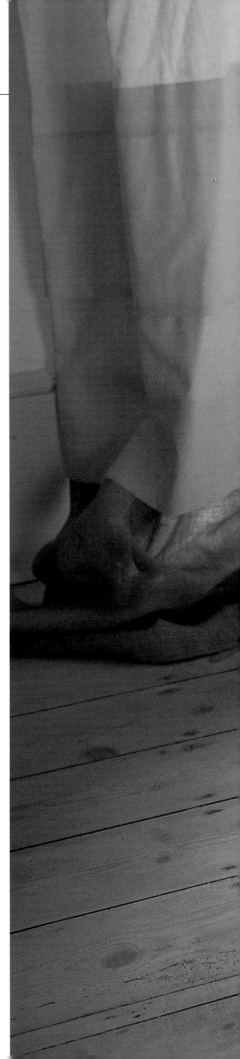

A matt or satin varnish preserves the soft look of the lime-washed effect.

limed effect floor

Focus on Technique

This paint effect is intended to enhance, not to disguise, the natural grain of the wood, so work in the direction of the grain throughout.

Materials and Equipment

centre punch and hammer

gloves, soft cloths and detergent

wood bleach and protective mask

floor sander, edging sander or hand sander

coarse and medium sandpapers

wire brush

white spirit

vacuum cleaner

oil-based eggshell in orchid white

white spirit

paint kettle and stirrer

satin oil-based varnish and flat varnishing brush

Preparation

Check the floor carefully for protruding nails or staples, and if necessary drive them in using a centre punch and a hammer.

1 Bleach out any stains or marks, then sand the floor using coarse, then medium grade sandpaper. Use an edging sander or hand sander for areas close to the walls.

2 Wire-brush the planks following the grain, working in sections to ensure none is missed. This will raise the grain and make a more absorbent surface to accept the paint. Vacuum the dust, then wipe over the entire floor with a cloth soaked in white spirit.

3 Dilute one part orchid white oil-based eggshell with two parts white spirit, and stir well. Using a flat varnishing brush, apply the paint quickly, always following the grain. Work on a few boards at a time, covering them from end to end. The paint will begin to dry in about 15 minutes.

4 Before the paint has dried completely, wipe back with a soft cloth, following the grain. Leave to dry for at least 1 hour.

5 Using a flat varnishing brush, paint on at least two coats of oil-based satin varnish.

geometric floor border

This border design is an example of a simple technique and form of decoration achieved in an unlikely choice of paint. Yet it is durable, practical and harmonious as well as dynamic and exciting. The square design was devised to echo the cubby-holes and finger-hole door pulls of the Rothko kitchen units on page 70.

The square has often been used by artists as an uncomplicated, rhythmical shape, conceptually balanced and straightforward, suggesting order and simplicity. It is an unchallenging motif which can be used to add colour and decoration while remaining timeless, unaffected by fads and fashion.

The paints used are silver and gold, which can appear as blue and yellow in certain lights. These complementary colours help to enhance and enliven the decoration of the rest of the room, and contrast well with each other. They also evoke the sun and sky, which are cheerful and uplifting associations to bring to an area of the room that often goes unnoticed.

Soft shades of blue and yellow offer a sympathetic embellishment to wooden floors and furniture, while the subtle metallic sheen adds a shimmer of elegant glamour to a plain pine floor.

A wide painted border around the centre of the floor defines the eating area, while the cool silvery blue complements the natural wooden furniture and the earth colours of the walls.

geometric floor border

Focus on Technique

The techniques used to achieve the floor border are simple and adaptable. The size and scale can be adjusted to any room and floor space. In a room like this, with two separate areas for cooking and eating, a border design can be used to unify the two. Depending on its position on the floor and the width of the painted band, it may also appear to widen or narrow the room. It can be used to create the illusion of a rug lying in the centre of the floor and the border colours can help to enhance or reflect the existing schemes. It is a cheap and flexible decorative device, where the introduction of metallic paint brings a suggestion of modernity and inventiveness to a plain wooden floor. The paint offers a hard-wearing finish with a subtle metallic sheen which can be buffed up if the floor becomes worn. The smooth, polished surface of the metal paint is pleasant to walk on with bare feet, and it will protect and seal the wooden floor against splintering and scuffs while still retaining the warmth of the wood.

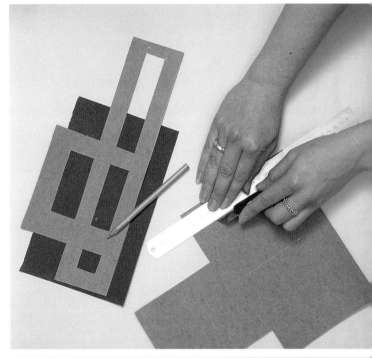

Materials and Equipment

sandpaper
fine wire wool
wire brush (optional)
tape measure
masking tape
craft knife
cutting mat
stencil card
pencil
steel ruler
oil-based metallic paints: pale gold, silver and antique
 gold
paintbrush
radiator roller and paint tray
satin or gloss acrylic floor varnish (optional)

Preparation

The floor should be sanded or rubbed down with wire wool to key the surface. If the wood is particularly impervious, work over it with a wire brush, working in the direction of the grain, before sanding the surface.

1

Plan the position of the border. Using masking tape, mask the edges of the narrow inner band and the wide outer band: these two sections will be painted first. Mask the edges of the alternate large and small squares in the wide band, always making sure to cut the tape straight across using a sharp knife so that the corners of the design are accurately formed.

2

On a sheet of stencil card, draw a small square stencil for the central motif and a band to fit the edges of the large square. Cut out the stencils using a craft knife and a steel rule, working on a cutting mat.

3

Paint the inner band pale gold and the wide band silver. Depending on the brand of paint you use, you may need to apply two coats to reach the required depth of colour and sheen. Allow the first coat to dry thoroughly before applying the second.

4

When the base colour of the wide silver band is dry, use the stencils to apply the small squares and borders in pale gold. Use the sponge head of a radiator roller to apply the paint, dabbing off any excess on the roller tray. Leave to dry.

5

Remove the masking tape and apply new tape to enable you to paint the central band in antique gold.

6

When all the paint is completely dry, gently rub over the whole surface with fine wire wool. You can apply satin or gloss varnish if you wish, so that the whole floor has the same sheen, but the paint will be quite hard-wearing without further protection.

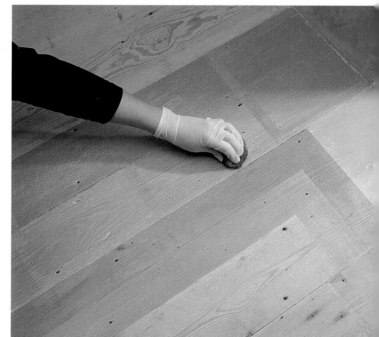

painted sisal rug

This ready-made sisal rug came in the colour of natural fibres which tend to show marks easily. The rug cried out for colour, and painting it was an easy way to introduce some warm colours into the room in an unobtrusive way. The decoration is a collage of different sections of colourwork in stripes, blocks and bands which all work with the woven lines of sisal. The warm honey-coloured yellows and ochres used for large areas of the design are balanced by contrasting lines and areas of brighter orange-reds and warm blue. The abstract design of the painted rug will work equally well seen from all sides; the final result is a hardwearing but individual floor-covering which injects a sympathetic addition of colour into the decorative scheme of the room.

The surface is easy to wipe clean and vacuum, and as sisal is fairly cheap, the rug is not too precious for everyday use.

The plain weave of the sisal rug, with its strong horizontal lines, suggested the simple blocks and bands of the painted design, using subtle washes of earth colours with accents of brighter red and cool blue.

Focus on Technique

The colour is applied as a series of thin washes. In this way you can easily control the depth of colour, and the thin paint will still allow the natural colour of the sisal to show through. The process can be used just as effectively to decorate fitted sisal carpeting.

Materials and Equipment

graph paper

pencil

chalk

tape measure

matt emulsion paints

paint kettles

matt emulsion glaze

medium and fine paintbrushes

gloves

flat oil-based varnish

varnishing brush

Preparation

Sisal rugs can be made up by binding the edges with a canvas border, or they may be whipped in wool. To make it easier to paint, the sisal should be brushed thoroughly with a wire brush to remove any loose fibre, then vacuumed.

1

Draw the design to scale on a piece of graph paper, and test samples of the colours you intend to use on a spare piece of sisal.

4

When the base colours are dry, begin to work in the details using smaller brushes. The base colours are mostly warm, with the details in contrasting cool colours and tones. It should not be necessary to use any tools to make straight lines as the weave of the sisal suggests lines to follow.

2

Mark out the design on the rug in chalk.

5

If at any point the paint begins to appear too dark, wash on a thin coat of off-white, leave to dry, then work over the section with a wash in another colour.

3

Mix up the colours you have chosen in plastic paint kettles. Each matt emulsion should be diluted 1:2 with matt emulsion glaze, then with a small amount of water. Begin by painting washes over the large areas. As each coat dries add another layer until the desired depth of colour is reached.

6

When the paint has dried completely, mix one part varnish with two parts white spirit and paint two coats over the whole rug. Leave at least 4 hours between coats. This will seal and protect the rug, but as the varnish is quite dilute it should not create too hard a finish to walk on.

canvas floorcloth

The design of this painted floorcloth was influenced by old coloured drawings of garden layouts, simplified into a muted, abstract design yet retaining the geometric shapes and the original gentle colour range of blues, greens and stones. The colours used have been layered in a series of thin washes, and textured to give an impression of depth and lushness to a flat surface.

The large areas of green and turquoise meet in softened edges to ease the eye from one colour to another, creating a harmonious mix. The details sitting on top are more sharply defined, but the paint surface has been sanded to soften them, so that they catch the eye without leaping too forcefully out of the overall design, or appearing as cut-out dark areas.

Canvas makes an economical and flexible but stylish floor covering and decoration. The painted surface is hard-wearing and easily maintained: it can be simply wiped clean with a damp cloth.

Fresh natural colours, inspired by grass, stone and water, merge and blend in muted harmony in this subtle floorcloth design. It creates a cool yet soft and comfortable decorative covering for a wooden floor.

canvas floorcloth

Focus on Technique

The technique introduces bold strong colours which appear muted and softened by the method of application. The canvas absorbs and holds the paint well, giving the colours depth and durability, while the final sanding allows the texture of the material to re-emerge.

Materials and Equipment

ready-made canvas floorcloth
paint roller and tray
white acrylic primer
tape measure
ruler
pencil
matt emulsion paint: greens, blues and cream
paint kettles
medium and fine paintbrushes
decorator's sponge
artist's brushes
fine grade wet-and-dry paper
matt acrylic varnish
varnishing brush

Preparation

Lay out the ready-made canvas floorcloth on a protected surface and use a roller to paint it with a base coat of white acrylic primer. Leave to dry.

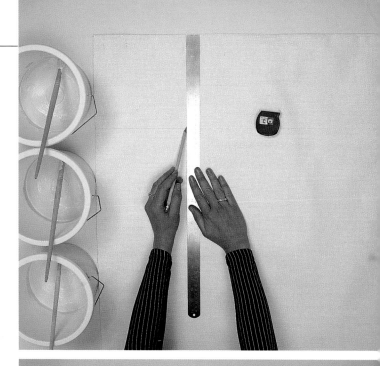

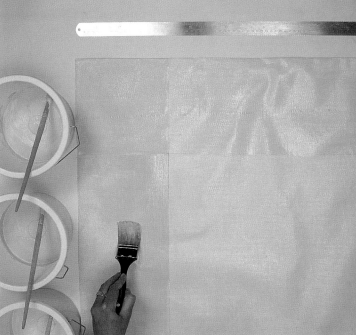

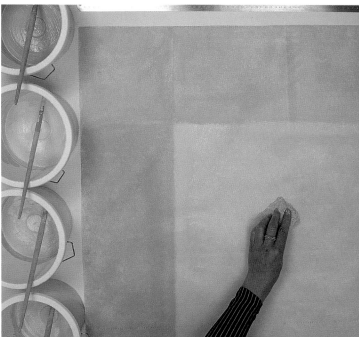

1

Measure and mark up your design in pencil. For this design, the cloth has been divided into a series of bands and squares.

2

For the first layer of colour, the paints should be diluted 2:1 with water. Apply using a brush and leave to dry.

3

Apply the colours for the next layer undiluted, using a damp sponge to give gentle variations of tone within each area of colour. Use a small paintbrush to work the paint up to the edges of the shape.

4

When the previous coat is dry, use the sponge again to add light washes of different greens over each area to mute the contrasting colours. Leave to dry.

5

Draw the decorative details using just a pencil, then paint in with darker colours using an artist's brush.

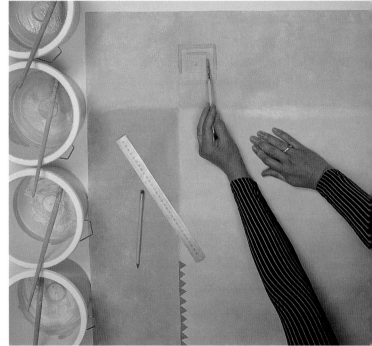

6

When the floorcloth is completely dry, sand all over the surface using fine grade wet-and-dry paper. To protect the floorcloth from wear and tear and give it a washable surface, paint the canvas with two coats of matt acrylic varnish.

special features

striped door surround

The simple rustic style of the striped door surround adds an unpretentious detail to the room and softens the hard lines of the doorway. The walls have been colourwashed in thin layers of yellow ochre acrylic to create a sense of warmth and cosiness despite the large proportions of the room, while the door and skirtings are painted in a warm, pale blue eggshell. A narrow, pale gold band around the door frame links it to gold detailing on the picture rail above and in other areas of the room. To form a visual bridge between the contrasting yellow and blue, the striped band is painted on a background of orchid white and built up in neutral shades.

All the colours are applied in a series of thin glazes, matching the translucent quality of the yellow washes on the rest of the wall. The success of the device relies on the combination of colours rather than the lavishness of decorative detail. The naive style of the rollered stripes and the soft, slightly irregular edge gives the decoration a relaxed look.

A painted border around the door, using light, neutral shades, forms a gentle transition in tone between the warm yellows of the wall and the contrasting pale blue door, while its simple straight lines find echoes in other decorative details in the room.

Focus on Technique

This form of decoration can be used to soften the abrupt lines of doorways and windows, and to change the visual proportions of an interior. Depending on the width of the band, it can help to suggest a wider, taller or shorter feature. The surround can also continue and emphasize the general colour scheme, tying in with decorative details elsewhere in the room.

Materials and Equipment

matt emulsion paint: orchid white and taupe
paint roller and tray
artist's acrylic paint: ochre, gold and raw sienna
paintbrushes
decorator's sponge
eggshell paint in pale blue
masking tape
foam radiator roller with short handle
paint kettles
matt emulsion glaze
ruler
pencil
stencil card
craft knife
cutting mat
fine grade wet-and-dry sandpaper

Preparation

The walls are colourwashed in three layers of yellow ochre over a base of rollered, orchid white matt emulsion. The woodwork is painted in a light, warm blue eggshell, with a band of lemon gold around the outer frame of the door.

3

Measure and cut the stencil for the stripes. Draw the cut-out stripe 4cm/1½in wide and long enough to fit across the painted band, leaving a 4cm/1½in border around three sides of the card. By cutting the border the same size as the stripe, you will be able to use it to position the stencil correctly.

1

Mask the edges of the door frame with tape, remembering to de-tack the tape first. Using a radiator roller and matt emulsion in orchid white, paint a band around the door frame. Keep the roller just clear of the frame: its width will determine the width of the band, giving a soft irregular edge. Leave this to dry.

4

To paint the stripes, mix some of the taupe glaze with a small amount of raw sienna acrylic paint. Fix the stencil in position with masking tape, aligning the first stripe with the corner of the door frame. Apply the colour with the roller while holding the stencil firmly in place. Paint all the stripes and leave to dry for about 1 hour.

2

The next colour is a glaze made by diluting one part taupe matt emulsion with two parts matt emulsion glaze. It should be rollered close to the door surround to allow a thin outer line of the base colour to show. Leave this to dry.

5

To add texture, lightly sand the finished surround using fine grade paper.

sandstone fireplace

The fireplace in this living room had a rather plain wooden surround, a little dull and lacking in weight and grandeur, and as the room's focal point it needed upgrading. One option would have been to remove it and fit a new stone surround, involving major upheaval and expense. The alternative solution was both quick and inexpensive: what looks exactly like an elegant carved stone fireplace is in fact the original wood, completely transformed through the ingenious use of textured paint and subtle colourwashes.

The first step was to improve the scale of the mantelpiece, and this was done by constructing a hollow block of MDF, both thicker and deeper than the original shelf. This gives a more weighty look to the whole fireplace, and the increased depth gives greater scope for a dramatic display of decorative objects. The plain shape is given depth and weight by the build-up of the stone-like texture and the stippled but smooth, layered surface. The finished effect feels warm and soft like real sandstone, and the introduction of 'natural' material to the room gives a timeless feel.

This skilful imitation of carved sandstone is achieved with astonishing ease and simplicity by mixing fine sand into masonry paint to create texture, then using subtle washes to reproduce the colour variations of natural stone.

Focus on Technique

This easy technique is flexible enough to allow a close colour match, but a real slab of stone could always be used as reference. Bear in mind, however, that the final coat of varnish will deepen the tone slightly.

Materials and Equipment

detergent
medium and fine wet-and-dry sandpaper
paintbrushes and undercoat
masking tape
fine sand
masonry paint in cream
decorator's sponge
artist's acrylic paints: white, burnt umber
  and yellow ochre
paint kettles
dusting brush and nailbrush
dead flat oil-based varnish and varnishing brush

1 Mix some very fine sand into a pot of cream masonry paint, and sponge this onto the surface. Use a fine brush for any recesses or corners.

Preparation

Degrease and sand down the fire surround and apply two coats of undercoat. Leave to dry, then lightly sand with fine grade wet-and-dry paper. Mask off the inner and outer edges with tape.

4 Sand the surface with medium grade wet-and-dry paper. Be careful not to round off the edges of the wood. The surface should feel velvety smooth when you have finished. Dust off.

2 Use a decorator's sponge to build up the surface texture, applying the paint with a stippling action. Leave this first coat to dry.

3 Still using the sponge and fine brush, add highlights and lowlights by mixing cream masonry paint with acrylic paint in white and burnt umber respectively. Leave to dry, then work back into the same areas again to enhance the effect.

5 Apply burnt umber acrylic paint to the bristles of an ordinary household nailbrush. Spatter the surface sparingly by gently pulling back on the bristles and directing the spatter carefully. Repeat the procedure with yellow ochre. Leave to dry.

6 Apply a coat of dead flat varnish which will seal the surface of the mock stone.

disguised cupboards

After numerous layers of wallpaper had been stripped off the walls of this bedroom, the unique textural quality of the old plaster became the basis of the redecoration. All the walls were textured and colourwashed to resemble the soft chalky surface, subtle variations and warm colouring of ancient plaster.

The room is to be a man's bedroom with a medieval style; with this in mind, a bold and simple symmetrical pattern was designed, using strong, unfussy lines. The large diamond motif is repeated all round the walls, and continues over the new floor-to-ceiling cupboards. These units are quite substantial and would otherwise have dominated the room. However, the strong graphic device distracts the eye and concentrates attention on the repeating pattern.

The apricot tones of the plaster are brought out more strongly in the diamond panels, using washes of burnt sienna. Gold paint has been added to give a subtle metallic finish to the diamonds, and this is picked up in the strong gold accent of the false dado, which forms a solid base line for the patterned section of the wall.

The subtle burnt sienna and gold design brings calm and order to the room while achieving its primary purpose, which is to make the new fitted cupboards appear unobtrusive and unified with the room.

disguised cupboards

Focus on Technique

The diamond panels are colourwashed using the same technique employed over the rest of the wall, with the addition of gold paint to give them an opalescent sheen. The dado is gilded using gold Dutch metal leaf.

Materials and Equipment

tape measure and chalk
chalk line or straight edge
masking tape
artist's acrylic paints: burnt sienna and bright gold
paint kettles
decorator's sponge
fine paintbrushes
matt emulsion paint in orchid white
acrylic gold size
Dutch metal leaf in gold
sharp scissors
clear button polish or shellac

Preparation

Measure the walls and units to ascertain the scale and number of diamonds that can be fitted around the room.

1 Mark the height and width of each diamond with chalk, then define the shapes. Use a chalk line if you have some assistance, or a long straight edge if working alone. Also mark a band 2.5cm/1in wide at the foot of the diamond panels, to act as a dado. Mask both edges of the band with tape.

4 Paint the dado band with acrylic gold size using a fine brush, and leave to dry for a minimum of an hour.

5 Cut strips of gold Dutch metal leaf with sharp scissors. Place each strip along the band, rub the back of the transfer paper gently, then peel it off.

2 Dilute some burnt sienna acrylic paint with water to make a thin wash. Use a sponge to apply the wash to the large areas, and a brush for the edges and points. The next layer is applied in the same way using a wash of gold acrylic. The dado band should be given a wash of burnt sienna only.

3 Dilute orchid white matt emulsion 2:1 with water and sponge on as a softening layer over the sienna and gold diamonds, leaving patches of the colours showing through. Make sure the sponge is rinsed frequently and used slightly damp.

6 When the band is completely covered, leave to dry, and protect it from tarnishing with two coats of clear button polish or shellac. This is quick-drying so you can apply the second coat within an hour of the first.

7 Remove the masking tape from the edges of the gilding. Gently pull the tape back against itself to prevent the edge ripping unevenly.

rothko kitchen units

The decoration of these kitchen units was inspired by the luminous colour and simplicity of the work of the painter Mark Rothko. His abstract paintings were an attempt to purify his work of all associative imagery and symbols, so that the observer could concentrate on the essence of colour and the emotional and spiritual responses it generates. The variables of colour, tone and depth of saturation help to create an inviting, stimulating atmosphere in the kitchen. The predominance of reds, coppers and golds imbues the scheme with a comfortable warmth which is also easy on the eye, due to the subtlety of the tonal variations and the careful combination of warm and cold hues.

The cupboards have been unified with bands of earthy metallic colours to bring an original, modern feel to the room. The depth of the colour gives the units a substantial solid look without appearing too heavy. The metallic sheen increases the vibrancy of the colour range, while the colours have been built up in thin layers to allow light to work through and reflect on the sheen beneath. This results in a resonant luxurious effect, with an arresting use of the light-reflective qualities of translucent paint. It expresses how cheerful and opulent deeper tones of colour can be.

These kitchen units have been given plain wooden doors painted in a variety of tones and colours within a limited range of hues. The underlying metallic sheen reflects the light as it hits each cupboard at a different angle, resulting in subtle colour changes and harmonies.

Focus on Technique

To ensure the perfect simplicity of the design, the existing unit carcasses have been fitted with replacement doors cut from 25mm/1in MDF board. Doors and drawers are opened by square cut-out pull-holes, and the paints and varnish are all very durable and scratch-resistant, making this technique ideally suited to the rigorous demands of the working kitchen.

Materials and Equipment

white acrylic primer and medium paintbrush
off-white undercoat
fine guage wet-and-dry sandpaper
rubber gloves
oil-based metallic paints: silver and pale gold
varnishing brush
fine-gauge wire wool
protective mask
damp cloth
artist's acrylic paints
paint-mixing container
sponge
masking tape
fitch
satin or gloss acrylic varnish

Preparation

Prime the bare MDF doors with two coats of acrylic primer and one coat of off-white undercoat. Allow each coat to dry thoroughly. Lightly smooth the surface between coats, using fine wet-and-dry sandpaper.

1 Wearing rubber gloves, apply a coat of oil-based metallic paint to the doors using a flat varnishing brush. To add interest to the final effect, paint alternate cupboards with silver and pale gold.

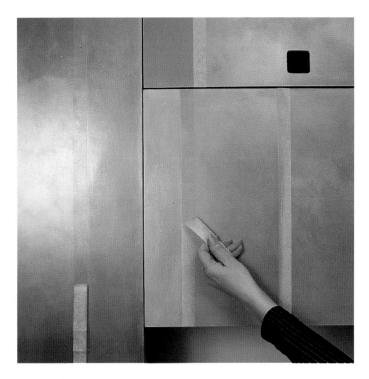

4 Choose the positions of wide contrasting bands on each door. Separate the bands with masking tape and apply alternate thin colourwashes of metallic paint. Allow to dry thoroughly before removing the tape.

2 When the metallic paints are completely dry, rub down with wire wool, using a circular motion. Wear gloves and a mask while working. Wipe the surface with a soft, damp cloth and leave to dry. If the paint seems too thin, apply a second coat and repeat the procedure.

3 Apply a series of colour wash layers using dilute acrylic metallic paints, with a sponge or a paintbrush. Use a selection of shades of red, copper and gold, varying the colours between each door. Allow to dry, and smooth with the fine sandpaper before applying the next wash.

5 Reposition the tape to mask the edges of the tape marks or the edges of the painted bands. Paint these narrow defining bands in deeper or brighter colours, using a fitch.

6 When all the paint is completely dry, remove the tape and smooth the surface gently using fine-gauge wire wool. Varnish the cupboards with several coats of satin or gloss acrylic varnish.

painted furniture

harlequin cupboard

The clean, classic lines of this modern cupboard offer the perfect opportunity for extravagant painted decoration. It has been given a double personality: the exterior is boldly patterned in a glamorous red and gold harlequin design, but the doors open to reveal the other side of its character – a jaunty stack of cubby-holes painted in a range of bright contrasting colours.

There is no hint of gaudiness in the design of the exterior decoration. The underlying red is a soft, deep terracotta, brushed over with a thin gold wash to integrate it with the stencilled gold diamonds. The metallic paint has a subdued glow and is given a soft sheen with a finishing coat of wax polish.

The same combination has been used on the front edges of the cubby-holes to relate the inside of the cupboard to its suave exterior. The paints used for the cubby-holes, though strong and bright, have all been chosen to relate well to the terracotta and gold of the outside when the doors are opened.

Deep but glowing tones of terracotta and gold in a stylish diamond pattern decorate the outside of this cupboard, which opens to reveal a surprising interior.

Focus on Technique

To achieve the thin wash of gold on the cupboard, gold powder is suspended in wallpaper paste. The gold diamonds are applied through a stencil; cut several stencils as the card gets damp with regular use.

1 Paint the outside of the cupboard and both sides of the doors with two coats of terracotta matt emulsion, keeping the brush strokes as even as possible. Leave to dry.

Materials and Equipment

medium and fine grade sandpaper
white acrylic primer
matt emulsion paint: terracotta and bright colours
paintbrushes and paint kettles
wallpaper paste and gold powder
measuring spoon
tape measure and steel rule
pencil and stencil card
craft knife and cutting mat
PVA glue
masking tape
decorator's sponge
satin or eggshell varnish and varnishing brush
clear wax polish and soft cloths

Preparation

Sand the cupboard and paint it with two coats of acrylic primer.

4 Mix one part PVA glue with two parts gold powder, then add a drop of water to get the consistency of thin cream. Attach the stencil to the cupboard with masking tape and begin to apply the diamonds, using a sponge. It is best to start in the middle and work out.

2 Mix up the wallpaper paste following the instructions on the packet. Mix approximately one part gold powder with three parts wallpaper paste and stir well. Using a series of long strokes, brush this paste mix onto the cupboard. Leave to dry, then apply a second coat if necessary.

3 Measure the height and width of the cupboard and work out the size of diamond needed to fit the dimensions neatly. Mark up the cupboard to help you position the stencil. Draw the diamond shape on stencil card and cut out using a craft knife.

5 When the gold is dry, varnish the surface with a satin or eggshell varnish and leave to dry.

6 Lightly rub down the cupboard with fine sandpaper, and apply a coat of good quality wax polish. Leave for 5 minutes, then polish off with a soft cloth.

gilded bedhead

A rectangular bedhead made from a panel of MDF needed a spectacular decorative treatment to make it visually satisfying in a room full of interesting and luxurious textures and complex colour. The gilded effect chosen is classic and simple, yet its clean, crisp lines also look refreshingly modern when imposed on the restrained, angular shape of the bedhead.

The gilded finish suggests opulence, but the use of copper over most of the bedhead makes for a very warm and inviting look that escapes looking brash. In the context of this bedroom, the pink tones of the copper link the bed with the warm apricot of the walls, while the gilt border picks up on the other gold details nearby, bringing a sense of unity to the whole room. Gilding with Dutch metal leaf is a durable and inexpensive way to turn going to bed into a sumptuous and indulgent experience.

Gold and copper coloured metal leaf are used lavishly in a simple, understated design to create a sophisticated piece of furniture.

gilded bedhead

Focus on Technique

Before applying the gilding, the bedhead is marked up in squares the size of a whole leaf. Butt the squares of metal leaf together carefully, as they are very thin and overlaps will be visible. If any areas of the gilding do not adhere properly it is possible to resize, leave to dry, then patch them, but you should try not to apply size over the areas already gilded as this will change the colour. Dutch metal leaf will tarnish over time unless it is varnished.

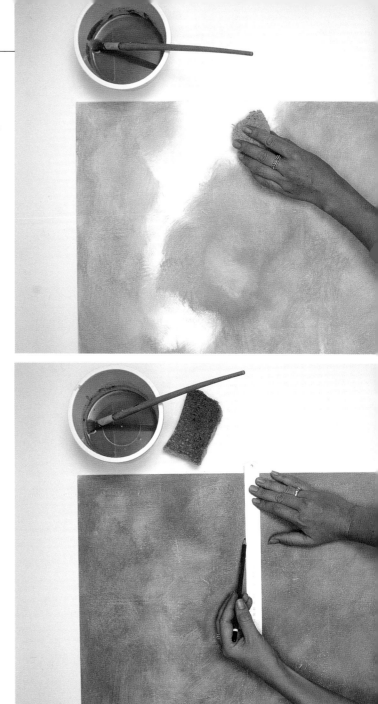

Materials and Equipment

white acrylic primer
paintbrush
fine grade wet-and-dry sandpaper
matt emulsion paint in terracotta
paint kettle
decorator's sponge
ruler
pencil
acrylic gold size
Dutch metal leaf in copper and gold
small artist's brush
soft cloth
dusting brush
clear button polish or shellac
flat varnishing brush

Preparation

The bedhead is made from MDF board attached to the bed by two wooden battens screwed to the back. Paint on two coats of white acrylic primer, then sand lightly to a smooth finish.

1

For the base colour, mix one part terracotta matt emulsion paint with two parts water. To avoid unnecessary brush marks, wash the colour onto the bedhead using a sponge. Apply two thin layers. Leave to dry.

2

Dutch metal leaf comes in 14cm/5in squares so, using a ruler and pencil, mark out the bedhead in a grid of 14cm/5in squares to help with positioning.

3

Paint the bedhead with an even coat of acrylic gold size. Make sure the whole surface is covered, and brush the size in well to avoid marks which might show through the thin metal leaf.

4

Leave the size to dry for at least an hour, then begin the gilding. Apply the copper leaf to the inner squares first. Butt the first sheet up to the line at one edge, then slowly lay it down, rubbing the back gently as you do so. When the copper squares are all in position, cover the border with gold leaf in the same way.

5

If any areas have been missed or the leaf has not fitted exactly, patch with smaller pieces. When the surface is covered, wipe off any loose leaf with a soft cloth and dusting brush.

6

Leave the size and gilding to dry overnight, then apply two coats of clear button polish or shellac. This is very fast-drying and must be applied quickly, so it is best to work in sections to avoid missing areas. Allow at least 30 minutes before painting on the second coat.

table-top border

A simple but solid pine kitchen table has been given a new style with the introduction of painted bands around the top which are echoed in the textured craquelure base and turned legs. The inner band of gold around the table top gives the decoration a warm glow and harmonizes well with the natural colour of the wood. The outer edge of the border is a bolder contrast with the wood: a band of almost white craquelure gives definition to the edge of the table. It is punctuated with small red squares to add colour and interest. The theme is carried down to the base which is decorated with a craquelure varnish over white primer. Details of the turned legs are enriched with occasional gold and terracotta painted bands. This pale treatment has the effect of refining the rather heavy legs, while the natural wood of the table top is left to harmonize with the wood floor and other natural materials in the room.

The solid and serviceable pine kitchen table is given a stylish edge by adding painted decorations in muted white, deep red and gold, with a craquelure finish.

Focus on Technique

The white band and table base have a two-part craquelure varnish. Follow the manufacturer's instructions, as these products vary. To assist the cracking process the varnish can be warmed with a hot air gun or hair dryer.

Materials and Equipment

detergent and gloves

sandpaper in various grades

ruler and pencil

masking tape

acrylic primer and paintbrushes

two-part water-based craquelure kit

artist's oil paint in burnt sienna

soft cloth

white spirit

matt emulsion paint in terracotta

gold metallic paint

stencil card

craft knife and cutting mat

satin or eggshell oil-based varnish

varnishing brush

Preparation

Clean and sand the table, then measure and mask off a band 6cm/2¼in wide, about 2.5cm/1in from the edge of the table and another band 6cm/2¼in inside that. Brush on two coats of acrylic primer, making sure the outer band is well covered. Treat the base of the table in the same way, using the same procedure to achieve the craquelure finish.

1 Apply the base coat of the two-part craquelure varnish. The liquid is very thick and must be applied quickly and evenly.

4 Remove the masking tape from the inner edge of the craquelure and re-mask, covering the inner edge to leave the next band ready for painting. Base this band with a coat of terracotta emulsion, leave to dry; then paint with a solid coat of gold paint and leave to dry.

2 Apply the top coat of the two-part varnish, following the manufacturer's guidelines on how long to allow between coats. The varnish used here is a quick-drying water-based product which must be allowed to dry thoroughly before the next step.

3 When the top coat is dry, brush on some artist's oil paint in burnt sienna and rub it into the cracks. After about half an hour when the paint is half dry, remove the excess with a cloth soaked in white spirit, wiping gently. Leave to dry overnight.

5 Measure, draw and cut a chequered stencil from card. Position it centrally over the two stripes and secure with masking tape. Apply the terracotta paint with a stiff brush, then remove the stencil and reposition until the border is complete.

6 When the paint is completely dry, apply two coats of satin or eggshell oil-based varnish using a flat varnishing brush. Lightly sand between coats with fine grade wet-and-dry paper.

chest of drawers

This chest of drawers has been decorated in a range of neutral and terracotta colours to create a gentle yet striking link with the graphic diamond motif on the bedroom walls. To create this effect, each surface has been textured before colourwashing and decoration. The patterns used are a patchwork of various simple repeated shapes, put together using colours that are sympathetic to the overall scheme of the room.

Each drawer is treated separately, as is each side, and here instructions are given for two drawers, as the other designs involve the same techniques. Sanding back the drawers has given them a muted look with a similar tone to the whole piece. The motifs used also reflect the painted design on the wall behind, anchoring the piece firmly in its setting.

Each drawer of the painted chest has been given an individual treatment, yet the design is unified by colour and pattern.

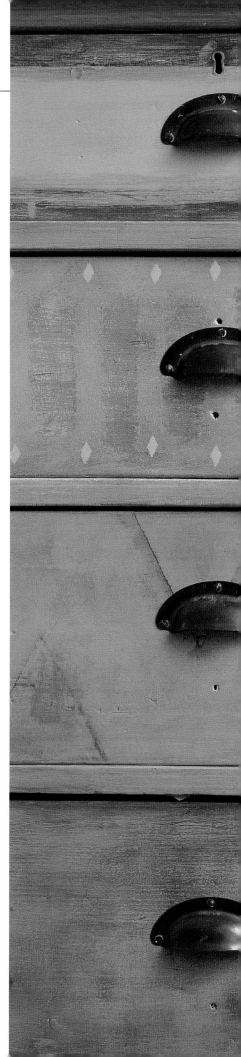

Focus on Technique

Each drawer has been decorated with a different geometric design, either hand-painted or stencilled.

Materials and Equipment

sandpaper

detergent

undercoat

paintbrushes

matt emulsion paint: cream, taupe and beige

crackle-glaze medium

decorator's sponge

artist's acrylic paints: burnt umber, yellow ochre, raw
  sienna and burnt sienna

artist's brushes

pencil, steel rule and stencil card

craft knife and cutting mat

matt varnish and flat varnishing brush

Preparation

Sand the chest, then paint with a thin layer of under-coat. When dry, paint the top, sides and each drawer in a selection of off-white colours, using different tones of cream, taupe and beige matt emulsion.

1 Paint the first drawer with an even layer of crackle-glaze medium over the off-white matt emulsion. Leave to dry. Apply a top coat of a different emulsion, brushing the paint on quickly with rough strokes to create texture. Leave to dry.

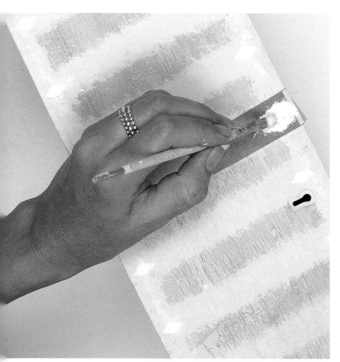

4 Draw and cut a stencil of a small diamond, then apply in a paler colour at the top and bottom of each stripe.

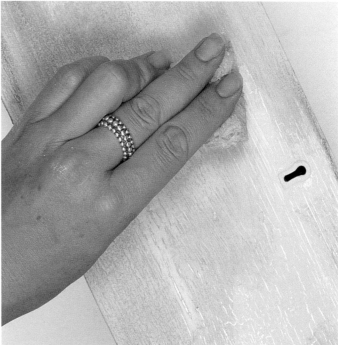

5 For the second drawer, brush on a coat of emulsion using thick paint applied roughly to create a textured surface. Leave to dry. Apply two thin washes of dilute raw sienna using a sponge.

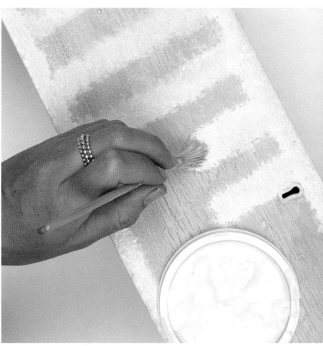

2 The paint should crack to expose the colour beneath and give an aged effect. Dilute some burnt umber acrylic with water, then wash over using a sponge. When part dry, wipe the surface again with a damp sponge leaving the colour in the cracks.

3 Measure the drawer and mark a series of evenly spaced vertical bands. Use a brush to stipple on the colour leaving an uneven edge. Two coats are applied, first off-white emulsion, then off-white with a touch of yellow ochre acrylic added.

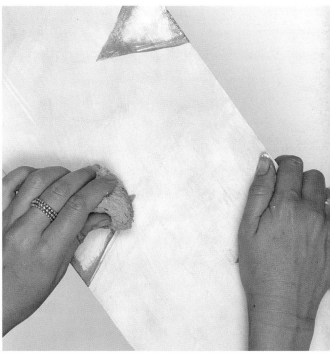

6 Using a pencil and ruler, measure and mark evenly spaced triangles across the top and bottom of the drawer. Paint with a solid coat of terracotta/red paint. Leave to dry, then apply another layer of watered-down paint.

7 While the paint is still wet, wipe the colour off again using a sponge: this should leave the shape as broken colour. Finally, rub over the whole surface using fine sandpaper. Finish with a protective layer of matt varnish, lightly sanding between coats.

opalescent mirror frame

A wide wooden frame around a small square mirror has been built up with gesso and filler until it takes on a three-dimensional effect and can be carved to give the impression of hand-crafted tiles or mosaic. Translucent colours built up in thin layers over the white base reflect light from the various planes, giving depth to this tapestry-like mix of rich hues. As a top coat, opalescent paints are added to heighten the light-reflecting effect. A whole rainbow of colours has been used, apparently at random, but warm colours have been alternated with cold ones throughout, so that each square in the pattern has equal weight and the general effect is finely balanced even though it is full of contrast.

The joy of this kind of project is that a simple, crude object can be treated in an original and creative way to become a precious and unique decorative piece and a focus of interest in a room.

Hand-carved square 'tiles' painted in rainbow colours make an arresting frame for a small mirror.

Focus on Technique

The frame surface is built up to a more or less uniform height, then marked out and carved to resemble tiles. The differences in height are quite small – try not to carve right back to the wooden frame.

Materials and Equipment

fine grade wet-and-dry sandpaper
masking tape
white acrylic gesso
paintbrush
all-purpose filler and small filling knife
pencil, ruler and craft knife
artist's acrylic paints in rainbow colours
  and opalescent finish
fine artist's brush and dishes for colour mixing
glass etching liquid
foam radiator roller head or stiff brush
wax polish and soft cloth

Preparation

Sand down the surface of the wooden frame and make sure it is dust-free. Mask off the edges of the mirror with tape.

1 Apply a couple of thin coats of acrylic gesso, leaving a few minutes' drying time between layers, then lightly sand with fine wet-and-dry paper. Then add a thin layer of all-purpose filler. Add successive coats, alternating gesso and filler. Leave to dry at each stage and lightly sand every couple of layers.

4 Brush over two more coats of gesso. Leave to dry, then sand lightly.

5 Paint the squares using acrylic paints in rainbow variety, alternating warm and cold colours. Thin the paints with water and apply them in washes.

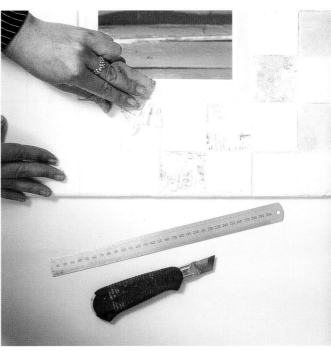

2 When the surface has reached a depth of about 5mm/¼in leave the frame to dry overnight. Fill any cracks and sand the surface smooth, then measure and mark out squares vertically and horizontally using a pencil and ruler.

3 Cut out alternate squares using a sharp knife and a filling knife. Try not to remove the filler right down to the frame base.

6 Apply a top coat of opalescent acrylic colours, painted on solid. Leave to dry before removing the masking tape from the mirror.

7 Mask an inner border and stipple frosting liquid onto the mirror, using a small foam roller head or a stiff brush. Apply wax polish to the painted frame and buff up with a soft cloth.

painted storage box

The boldly arresting decoration given to this old box has breathed new life into it. The warm, earthy base colours are contrasted with blocks and panels of different complementary blues, greens and aquamarines. The cheerful, abstract design is an uncomplicated combination of solid paint and more transparent washes, resulting in a vital mix of texture and colour. When sanded, the character of the wood is brought back into play to add its texture to the design, and the colours are somewhat softened.

The box originally had a heavy, clumsy character and had multiple wood stains, giving the wood an ugly appearance. The addition of the bright colours and random painted panels has visually changed its shape and lightened the overall feel without any structural work. It can now be used as a useful storage box and as a cheerful item of furniture.

Large blocks of colour are broken up with small areas of more detailed painting, and given extra interest by sanding the paint back until the natural wood grain begins to re-emerge.

Focus on Technique

The large flat areas on the top and sides of the box have been broken up by bold blocks of colour, and enlivened by smaller motifs and borders in contrasting or toning colours. Structural details, such as the joints at the corners and the edges of the lid, are emphasized with strong contrasts.

1 Mix some burnt umber acrylic paint with white emulsion, and apply the paint thickly to edges and details. Repeat using raw umber.

Materials and Equipment

coarse and medium wet-and-dry sandpaper
acrylic primer
paint kettle
paintbrushes
artist's acrylic paints
white emulsion paint
dishes for colour mixing
decorator's sponge

Preparation

Sand the box down well, then prime with acrylic primer diluted with water 2:1.

4 Add flashes of bright colours by painting a contrasting band or block of colour over the earth colours used as base colours.

2 Add further details with a mix of ultramarine and white emulsion paint.

3 When the previous colours have dried, deepen areas here and there with washes of acrylic paint applied with a damp sponge and brush. The acrylic colours should be diluted slightly with water.

5 Work back into areas here and there to emphasize colours with more washes.

6 Using coarse and medium grade sandpaper, sand the whole surface to give an aged look. The thick paint should be sanded unevenly to appear worn away in areas.

découpage leaf chest

The leaf chest has the poetic quality of a special place for storing memorabilia and objects of particular sentimental value. In itself, it is also a record of a pleasant walk in a beautiful place where the leaves were collected. Each leaf has been colour copied to capture its unfaded colours as they were on the day it was found.

Natural shades of plant papers and neutral off-whites dulled by the wash of burnt umber and varnish are a compatible background for the mix of green leaves with the occasional flash of hotter autumnal reds and browns. The soft layers of irregularly torn paper pieces sit behind the sharper, cut-out shapes of the simple square and rectangular backgrounds for the leaves and stems.

Previously lacking in texture and character, the original box has been dramatically transformed and now adds a touch of soft, delicate interest to a neglected corner or wall.

Focus on Technique

The paper is built up in thin layers and sealed well, so it appears as a thick covering, yet is smooth and flat to touch. The paper should be evenly applied as it dries tightly with some shrinkage when laminated. This can be especially useful if stripping has weakened the box and it needs holding together.

1 Tear pieces of scrap paper into random shapes and sizes. Mix the PVA glue 1:2 with water and coat an area of the box. Apply the paper shapes beginning with the thickest first, always covering well with glue to ensure it is soaked in.

Materials and Equipment

sandpaper
metholated and white spirit
PVA glue
colour copies of a variety of freshly picked leaves
coloured and white cartridge paper
handmade and plant papers
thin papers, including tissue paper – preferably acid free and unbleached
varnishing brush and small artist's brush
scissors
craft knife and cutting board
cream matt emulsion
burnt umber oil paint
oil-based varnish, satin or eggshell finish
paint kettles

Preparation

Colour copy a selection of freshly picked leaves.To get the best result place them face down on a sheet of acetate then cover with sheets of white paper. Sanding and then cleaning the box with metholated spirit will ensure that the various papers adhere well to the surface.

4 Using an artist's brush and cream matt emulsion paint a variety of decorative boarders onto the leaf backgrounds. Leave to dry.

2 Cover the whole surface with a layer of tissue paper pieces. Being very thin, they can be overlapped to add stength and texture to the box.

3 Using scissors and a sharp craft knife, cut out the colour copies of the leaves. When the glue is completely dry on the box arrange the leaves in your chosen design. To give more depth and decoration glue the leaves to rough torn squares and rectangular pieces of coloured paper.

5 Dilute the varnish with white spirit 1:2 and brush on one coat, making sure that it does not run. Leave to dry.

6 Make a glaze of burnt umber oil paint and white spirit. Brush this over the surface, then wipe back with a soft cloth after 5-10 minutes. Varnish the box again when the oil paint is completely dry.

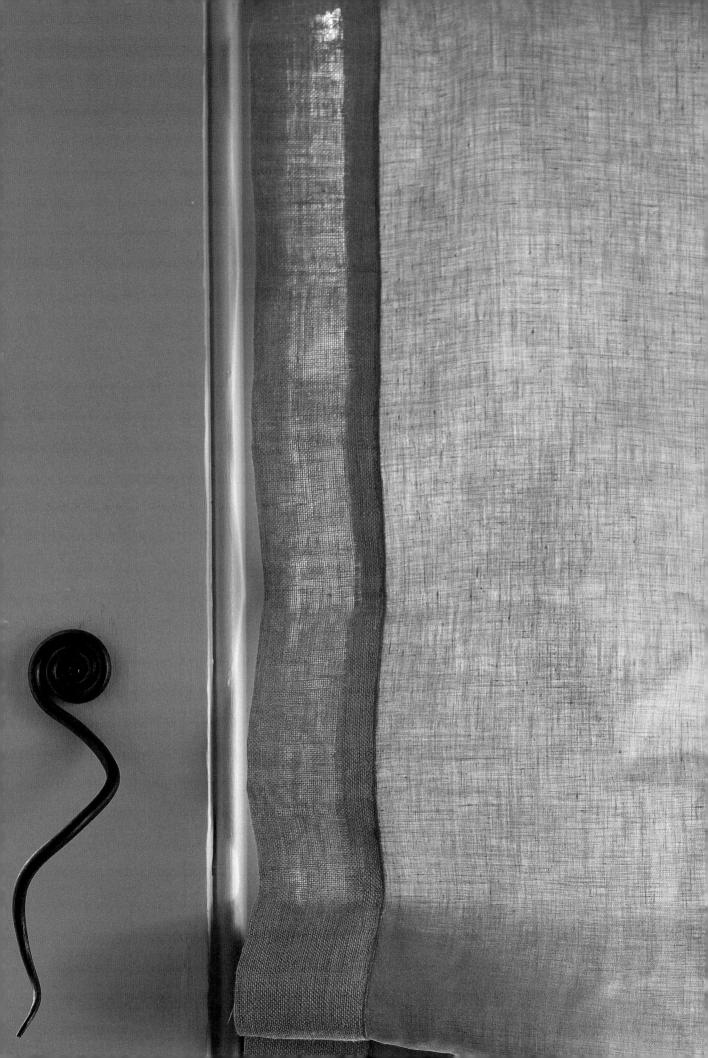

fabulous fabrics

handpainted curtains

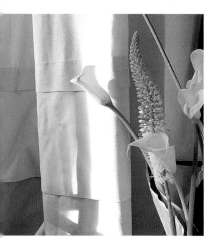

Oversized curtains always look wonderful, sweeping the floor and falling in generous folds, especially at a large window. For this room full of soft colours, natural materials and interesting textures, calico is the ideal fabric. Unbleached, its natural soft cream colour filters the light kindly, and any slight irregularities in its weave add to its appeal. It is so cheap that it can always be used lavishly, whatever the window size.

The addition of colour and some simple structure transforms this basic, workaday fabric into something quite elaborate and sophisticated. These full curtains have been made with several wide, horizontal pleats near the bottom, and a skirt of pre-shrunk hessian which sweeps the floor. The calico pleats have been coloured in fabric dyes in subtle graduated shades starting with light gold and shading down to the hessian at the foot.

The broad hessian band is doubly functional: it gives the curtains actual as well as visual weight, improving their hang, and it is the ideal fabric to have at floor level as it will not show the dirt.

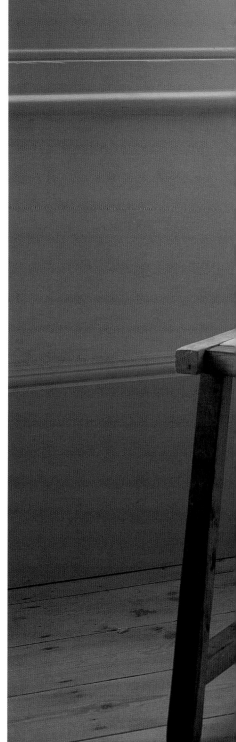

An original treatment for plain calico curtains: wide horizontal pleats in gentle colours and an overlong hessian 'skirt' to trail elegantly on the floor.

Focus on Technique

Though the painted pleats make the curtains look quite complex, they are extremely easy to sew from single lengths of wide fabric, simply stitching on the final band of hessian at the hem. Before painting on the dyes, the pleats are interleaved with a strip of lining paper to avoid any seepage of the dye. The paper can be moved along as each part of the pleat is painted and ironed dry.

Materials and Equipment

calico curtains with wide horizontal pleats
   and hessian band at hem
plastic sheeting and clean lining paper
fabric dyes: pale gold, antique gold and bronze
plastic mixing containers
paintbrushes
spare, clean fabric for ironing, and iron

Preparation

The calico curtains have been made to order with a skirt of pleated fabric dropping almost to the floor, trimmed with a broad band of hessian. Lay the curtain flat on a work surface covered with plastic sheeting and clean paper.

1 Tuck a sheet of lining paper under the first pleat to protect the rest of the curtain. Mix the palest dye with a small amount of water and paint it on in quick successive washes.

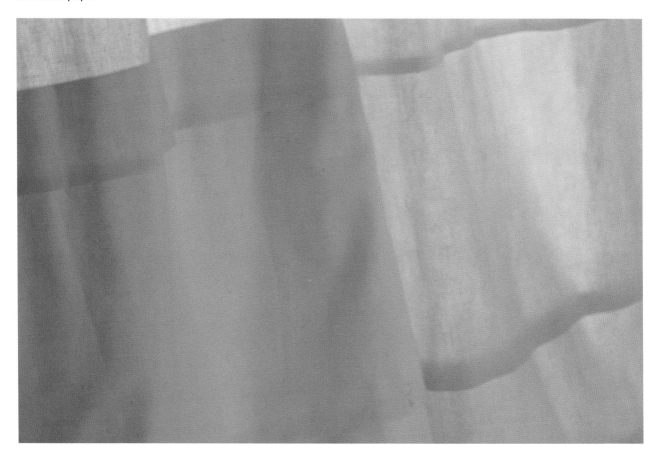

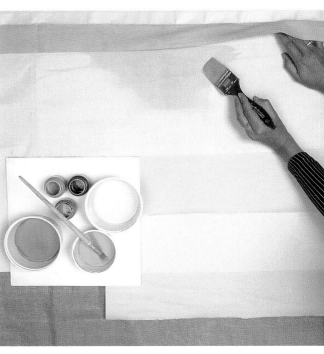

2 Lay a strip of clean fabric over the painted area and iron lightly to fix the dye.

3 When the first pleat is complete, rearrange the curtain on the flat surface and apply the next colour in the same way. Try to ensure that the wet dye does not touch any of the other pleats.

4 Use the dye nearest in tone to the colour of the hessian for the lowest pleat.

5 When all the pleats have been painted and have part-dried, the fabric can be flipped over and ironed again on the back to fix the dye.

painted roman blind

This room is decorated in sunny ochres and golds combined with neutral shades. Natural materials and textures and organic, simple shapes characterize the furniture and accessories. A simple, unfussy window treatment is demanded, using a natural fabric which will diffuse the light gently. For this small window, unbleached linen has been made up into an unlined and unstructured Roman blind which is inexpensive to make and can be made to fit any space. The blind draws up in neat, loose folds to allow maximum light through the window on a dull day. When in use it is fine enough to provide gentle shade without darkening the room too much, but thick enough to screen the view from outside effectively.

To warm up the neutral colour of the linen, it has been painted with fabric dyes in a warm range of earth colours: copper, reds and taupe brown. These have been painted on in quick washes diluted with water which means that the translucency of the fabric is unaffected. The effect of the dyes varies depending on whether the light is behind the blind or reflecting on the surface. They appear stronger at night, as natural light dilutes the strength of the washes.

Warm, earth-coloured dyes washed thinly over a neutral linen blind give a warm glow to the whole room when used to diffuse the daylight.

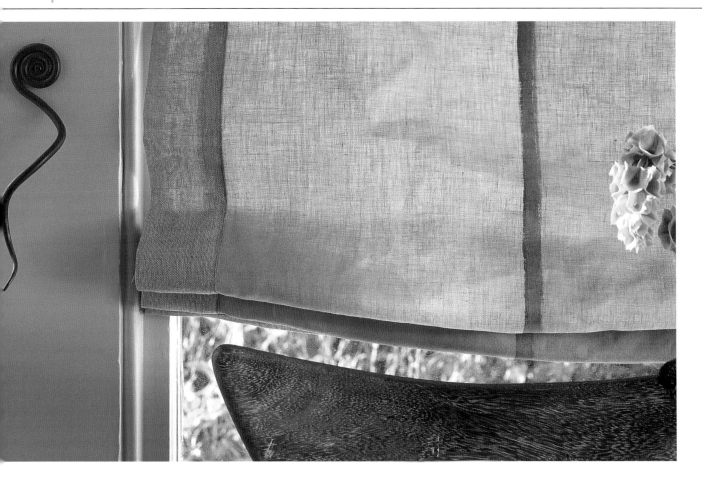

Focus on Technique

A simple and practical Roman blind can be made to match any room, using fabric dyes which are fixed with an iron. Test the effect of the dyes on a scrap of fabric before starting the blind. The painted material can be dry cleaned.

Materials and Equipment

unbleached linen (or ready-made blind)
tape measure
steel rule and pencil
iron
water-based fabric-painting dyes in earth colours
plastic mixing containers
plastic sheeting and large sheets of clean paper
large and small paintbrushes
hessian border fabric, needle and matching thread
Roman blind fittings

Preparation

Either buy a ready-made blind or paint the fabric first, then iron and attach a pre-shrunk hessian border, rings and cord. The blind is attached to the top of the window frame using a velcro strip.

3 Paint the other side in the same way using a different warm colour. Leave the two colours to dry for an hour, then turn the blind over onto a clean piece of fabric and iron the reverse.

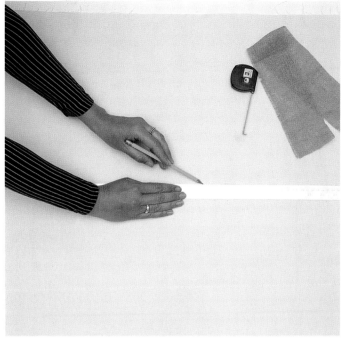

1 Measure the width of the fabric and mark a central stripe: the width of a ruler is perfect.

2 Dilute two parts fabric dye with one part water. Cover a flat work surface with plastic sheeting and clean paper. Spread out the linen and paint quickly with regular strokes down one side of the central stripe.

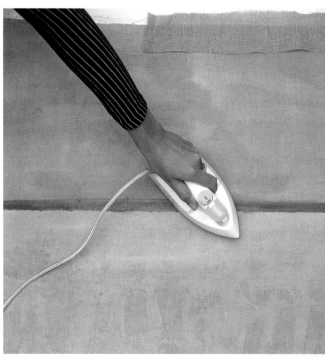

4 Turn the fabric back over and paint the central band using a smaller brush.

5 Allow to dry, then fix the dye by ironing on the reverse as before. Complete the blind by stitching on a hessian border and attaching the blind fitments.

polo lampshade

A plain parchment lampshade is given a radical new look with some fifties-style decoration, turning it from a rather boring, if functional object into a prominent feature of the room. The elements of the design are put together with a casual approach, tearing the shapes from coloured tissue and metallic foil. The roughly torn edges and irregular margins give the simple design an appealing vitality and turn this simple lampshade into a unique handmade piece. The colours change dramatically when the light is switched on. When lit, the shade gives a warm, orange-tinted light, but unlit during the day the colour scheme is mainly a combination of taupe and pink, with touches of shiny silver. Most of the papers used are thin and translucent to allow the light through and give a colourful effect, but some of the applied circles have been cut from denser paper and thin foil so that they show up dramatically when the shade is lit from within.

By night, the pink and brown tissue decorations cast a fiery, dramatic light.

Focus on Technique

Place the glued squares of tissue on the lampshade by eye, to give an improvised, handmade look: the decoration will appear more individual if imperfections are allowed. If the squares are too uneven you can quickly remove and replace them before the glue dries. It is important to remember to attach the paper only to the outside of the shade to avoid risk of fire.

Materials and Equipment

plain cylindrical lampshade

tape measure

selection of coloured handmade tissue papers

steel rule, pencil and scissors

bottle and jar lids

aluminium foil

PVA glue and brush

mixing container

clean paper

Preparation

Buy a lampshade with a simple shape, and gather a variety of handmade coloured tissue papers.

1 Measure the circumference and height of the shade to decide on the size of the squares, allowing for narrow margins between them.

4 Fold the circles in half and tear or cut out the centres to make ring shapes.

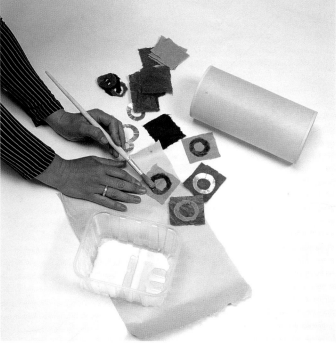

5 Dilute two parts PVA glue with one part water. Stick the circles on to the centres of the squares, alternating the colours each time, and place the squares on a flat surface to dry.

2 Measure and tear the squares against the edge of a steel rule. Use several different coloured papers.

3 Draw circles around bottle and jar lids, and tear or cut these out of different papers, including aluminium foil.

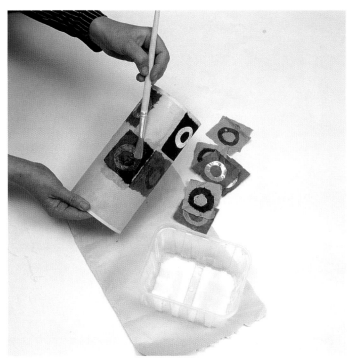

6 Turn the squares over on a clean sheet of paper and glue the backs. Place them by eye on the lampshade and smooth the tissue carefully with the glue brush. Leave to dry.

garden magic

iridescent furniture

Pretty wrought-iron chairs and a small matching table have been painted in intense but ice-cool colours to contrast sharply with their white and cream surroundings on the patio. On bright days these colours hold their own amid the vivid greenery of the foliage around the patio and the brilliant colours of summer flowers. Metallic paints add an extra brilliance, so that the furniture literally sparkles in the sunshine. The painted ironwork is fun and stimulating to look at, providing an oasis of refreshingly cool aqua colours, like a pool of blue water. The table top has been given a wash of pale blue to provide a quiet foil for the sparkling metalwork. The alternating combinations of greens, blues and purples emphasize the whimsical nature of this furniture, with its delicate curls of wrought iron.

Curly iron chairs become an amusing but not dominant feature of the patio when decorated with multicoloured metallic paints.

Focus on Technique

The bright shiny paints will help reflect heat and
protect the chairs from corrosion and weathering.
Remove any existing rust before beginning to
paint. Red oxide primer also helps to inhibit rust.

Materials and Equipment

gloves

wire wool

red oxide metal primer

paintbrushes

white spirit

metallic acrylic paints: green, blue, purple
   and turquoise

Preparation

Wire wool the metal furniture to remove any loose
flakes of paint and rust.

1 Prime the furniture with red oxide metal primer.
Make sure every surface is well covered as the primer
will help protect against the return of rust in the
future. Clean the brush with white spirit.

2 Paint alternate curls and scrolls with green metallic paint. Use a fitch brush carefully to ensure the colours meet neatly.

3 Paint a third scroll in bright blue.

4 Complete the chair back with purple metallic paint.

5 Paint the back frame in blue, and continue to alternate colours over the rest of the furniture.

sandstone floor

The existing surface of this patio was self-levelling concrete which had been scored to suggest paving. Over time the concrete had darkened, and the result was a dead-looking surface which absorbed light and looked dull and dusty.

The aim of the paint treatment was to lighten the whole area by restoring a light-reflective surface, and to give the suggestion of sandstone, which marries well with the cream and white wall surrounding the patio, and looks warm and cheerful even on days when the sun is not shining. Masonry paint is applied in layers, resulting in a hard-wearing finish which is not easily distressed. The underlying concrete, although an ugly colour, has a hardwearing and satisfying texture which mimics stone slabs quite well and absorbs the paint to give good adherence.

Ordinary concrete, which has fortunately been scored to resemble paving stones, is painted to look like costly sandstone slabs.

Focus on Technique

When applying paint to this surface it is necessary to build up layers rather than putting on just one thick coat which will chip easily. The simplicity of the technique means it would be possible to rework layers of different colours and spattering to achieve a depth and colour similar to real stone. The absorbency of the concrete is helpful in creating the stone effect.

Materials and Equipment

hosepipe with jet-spray attachment
stiff brush
masonry paint in two off-white shades
paint kettles
paintbrushes
universal stainers: yellow ochre and burnt umber
decorator's sponge

Preparation

Clean the patio floor by jet-blasting with a powerful hose, then brushing it down with a stiff brush.

3 Mix a little of one colour paint with yellow ochre universal stainer and another with burnt umber. Dip a stiff brush in one mix at a time, and spatter the slabs individually with large and small dots. Wipe over with a wet sponge lightly when nearly dry.

1 Dilute two different off-white shades of masonry paint. The paint should be quite thin, diluted 1:3 with water, to allow it to flood the concrete floor. Work the wash into every hole and crack using a big brush. Try to chequer the floor, alternating the colours.

2 Using thicker paint mixes, alternate the colour again but this time use a dry-brushing method, applying the paint mostly to the edges and the prominent parts of the textured surface.

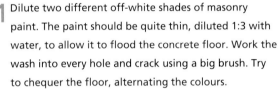

4 Mix a drop each of the ochre and umber stainers with some cream masonry paint. Using a fine brush, apply this darker colour along the grooves between the concrete slabs. These lines will darken over time as they accumulate dirt and possibly moss or lichen, so keep the painted line fairly light.

painted wall and arbour

The purpose of this design was to introduce Mediterranean colour and style to a patio which looked a bit bleached out and in need of a focus. The colours are chosen to be harmonious and mellow, interesting without being too garish, as the patio is viewed all year round from large windows and doors. The colours suggest that the wall and bench are bathed in warm sunlight even on a cloudy day. The white border design gives an accent to the cream bands and emphasizes the shapes of the bench and the simple, arched *trompe l'oeil* which follows the outline of the arbour.

The metal arbour has been repainted in masonry paints to match the colours of the wall and bench. Garden furniture usually comes in a choice of white, black or green, often with a glossy finish to give better protection against corrosion, but here, the alternative use of masonry paint means the piece can be matched to its surroundings with a matt finish. The paint can be freshened whenever the walls are repainted, unless plants have taken over by then. The border motif is a simplified version of a style of decoration often used around the doorways and windows of Indian, Moroccan and African houses, where it is drawn or painted in lime- or chalk-based paints.

The different styles of the stone bench, wooden tubs and metal arbour are unified by a simple, fresh colour scheme of sand, cream and white, with a central blue panel which echoes the shape of the arbour and provides a strong focal point.

Focus on Technique

The wall render was mixed with sand to produce a soft ochre colour. Where the colour appeared uneven it was unified by washes of durable masonry paint with ochre stainer added. This paint is easy to tint, making colour coordination simple and it has been used again for the metal arbour. The most important consideration is preparing the surfaces to be painted.

Materials and Equipment

masonry paint: various shades of cream and white
paint kettles
paintbrushes
universal stainers: ochre and blue
ruler and pencil
stencil card
craft knife and cutting mat
masking tape
radiator roller head
artist's brush
wire wool
white oil-based all-purpose undercoat

Preparation

The wall and bench were coated with a sand and cement render. Even up the colour of the render with a dilute wash of masonry paint stained to a similar colour. Paint the wall and bench with a series of bands in light to dark creams. On the back wall, paint bands so that they follow the shape of the arbour, and add washes of two blues onto the central panel.

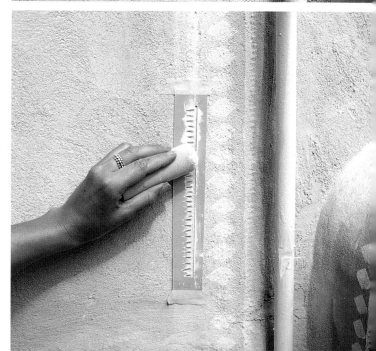

3

Use an artist's brush to apply white dots between the diamonds to complete the design.

1

Measure, draw and cut out a series of regularly spaced diamonds on stencil card. Place the stencil in the centre of the cream band and hold in place with masking tape. Use the sponge head of a radiator roller or a brush to apply white masonry paint, then move the stencil and repeat.

4

Rub down the arbour with wire wool, dust off and paint with a coat of oil-based all-purpose undercoat. When the undercoat is completely dry, paint over it with cream masonry paint. This will probably need to be done in two coats. Use a small brush for areas that are difficult to reach. Leave to dry.

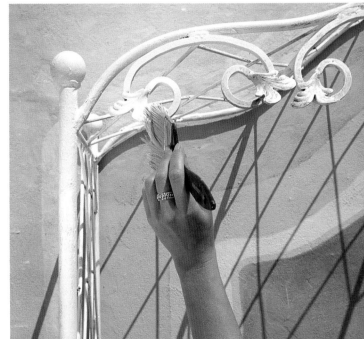

2

Cut a second stencil for the edging, which will appear as a series of white dashes, and apply this as before, again using white paint. Paint the design by hand around the curves in the border.

5

To enhance the shapes, pick out the details in white masonry paint. A small brush is essential for this to keep the paint neat. Apply a second coat if necessary.

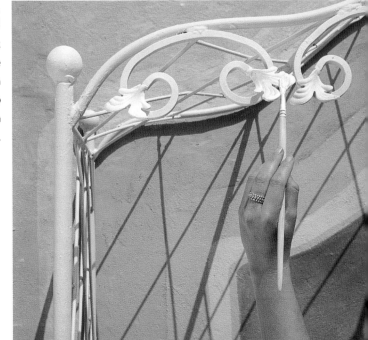

garden wall border

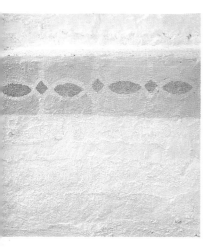

It's easy to forget that garden walls can be decorated with many of the same techniques that are used on indoor surfaces. On this wall beside a patio, a junction of two walls forms a convenient shelf for potted plants and other interesting garden paraphernalia. As all the walls are painted white, a stencilled border design defines the change of level at this point and links into other blue features around the patio.

The blues used are warm and luminous, giving a cool resting place for the eye when the impact of the sun is at its height on the white walls. The same stencil has been used twice, with a slightly muted light and dark blue first, then a brighter colour on top. The stencil was slightly misplaced the second time to give the design an edge like a tile. The border peeks through the greenery in summer but is exposed in winter when the foliage has died back.

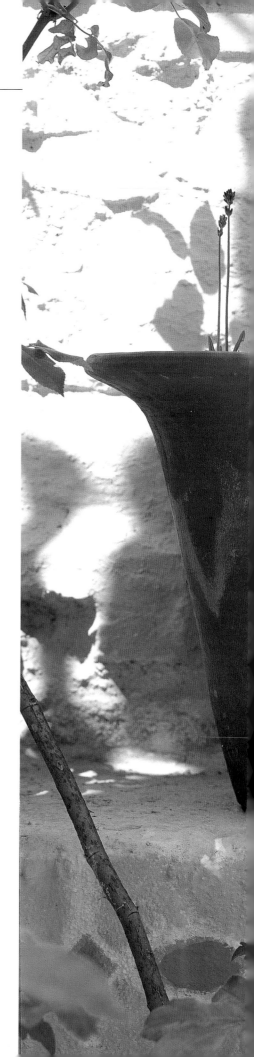

In summer when the plants are in full growth, the stencilled border is glimpsed tantalizingly through the greenery.

Focus on Technique

When decorating a rough-textured garden wall, there is no point in trying to be too exact about the design: any minor imperfections in the stencilling simply add to its charm.

Materials and Equipment

wire brush or stiff household brush

masonry paint: white and dark cream

paintbrushes

length of wood

steel rule and pencil

stencil card

craft knife and cutting mat

masking tape

paint kettle

blue universal stainer

decorator's sponge

stencil brush

Preparation

Remove any loose paint on the wall with a wire brush or stiff bristle brush, then paint with white masonry paint.

1 Measure, mark and then paint a band of deep cream masonry paint. Use a length of wood to help keep your line straight. Draw and cut out the design from stencil card, using a craft knife on a cutting mat.

2 Position the stencil on the wall and secure with masking tape. The first colour is a light mix of white masonary paint with a drop of blue stainer. Apply it with a sponge, stippling through the larger areas of the stencil.

3 Leave the stencil in place and apply a darker blue colour to the smaller cut-out areas using a stencil brush.

materials and equipment

As a rule, less is more. It is better to feel at ease with a few familiar and accessible tools than to assemble a collection of expensive equipment which might inhibit your freedom of expression by distracting you and dictating your way of working. Practically every project in this book can be achieved with just a decorator's sponge, a flat varnishing brush and a couple of fitches. A pencil and ruler are helpful but not essential and it is surprising how much measuring can be done by eye. The paints used are widely available and usually water-based, which assists easy colour

1 fitches
2 artist's brushes, flat fitch with angled bristles and sash brush; **3** flat varnishing brushes (gliders); **4** dusting brush and general purpose household paintbrush

matching and mixing. The patterns are basic and simple to achieve. This leaves a lot more time for the personal touch, the unique individual quality brought to an idea by the particular use of colour, texture and pattern. The special touch is often a more complex and layered process than an onlooker might realize, but every extra bit of effort and work will ensure the individuality of the result.

It is not the case that the simplest effect is the easiest to achieve – it is often the reverse. Much fudging and extraneous detailing can be used as a camouflage for badly executed techniques. If the actual paint effect used is flexible and creates an arena of developing possibilities, the sense of fun and excitement will show. Love of the work is more important than having the right brush or extender medium. Focus of intent, and being happy and relaxed while you work, are crucial. This list is not definitive, it is intended as a guide to the variety of equipment and materials you could use.

Acrylic gesso
Ready-made gesso is available for preparing surfaces and is usually of good quality. Follow the manufacturer's guidelines for its proper use.

Brushes
A wide range of brushes is available. A good guide is to assess the amount of bristles, as the more bristles in the brush the more paint it will hold. For greater control it is better to have fewer bristles and therefore a flatter brush. Choosing the appropriate size is more important. Smaller brushes are unlikely to carry much paint but are very useful for colour mixing. Flat varnishing brushes, or 'gliders', are perfect for most effects and give a smooth finish in all flat painting. They range in size from 1–15cm/$\frac{1}{2}$–6in. Fitches are invaluable for cutting in, edges and awkward corners. Buy artist's brushes from a good stationer's, art shop or craft supply shop. When choosing it is always best to describe the project and get advice from the stockist as brushes can vary in price hugely. Look after your brushes carefully (see page 140).

Button polish (shellac)
Various grades are available, with colours ranging from brown to bleached shellac (white polish). It is quick-drying. Use methylated spirit for thinning and cleaning brushes.

Carbon paper, tracing paper
Both are always helpful for stencil and design work.

Card
Stiff card can be used for 'carding' textured effects and can be prepared for use as sample board. Stencil card is

flexible and strong, but it will eventually distort as it becomes damp, so it is a good idea to cut several copies of a design if you are going to use it many times.

Cloths and rags

A generous supply of lint-free rags is needed for general cleaning and for wiping back paint. Stockinette cloth or old T-shirts are ideal.

Crackle-glaze mediums

These vary greatly: two-part water-based versions are now available for creating craquelure; the easier but less refined crackle-glaze can be used in the prescribed way or just as a texturing effect to create an interesting background for colour and pattern. Always read the instructions and do tests on sample boards.

Decorator's sponge

The decorator's sponge used in the book is the strongest and most freely available. It can be cut down to a size appropriate for the job and cut into shapes to use for a bold stamp effect. When picked out a bit it can be used much like a real organic sponge and is easy to clean and store.

Dust sheets

Use plastic sheeting or old cotton sheets to protect surfaces against paint spillages, dust and scratches.

Fabric paints

The range of colours and finishes available is now greatly improved, with a variety of options. The most useful are water-based and can be fixed by ironing.

Kitchen and household tools

A kitchen whisk and a fine mesh strainer can both be helpful when preparing special colour mixes, while an ordinary spoon is invaluable for adding small amounts of paint to a mix. A screwdriver makes a good paint tin opener. Use a household nailbrush for spattering paint.

Knives

Use a sharp craft knife for cutting stencils. A cutting mat with a resealable surface is ideal and will not blunt the blade. The most flexible filler knives are often known as continental filler knives: they vary slightly in style. They may need to be bevelled before use (see page 20).

Masking tape

This comes in a variety of sizes. For use on walls or over new paintwork it is always

1 black and white photocopies
2 carbon paper 3 tracing paper
4 graph paper 5 leaves stuck onto hand-made paper, ready for photocopying
6 design drawn through carbon paper
7 cutting mat 8 colour photocopies
9 fitches 10 stencils 11 radiator roller sponge head 12 cut-down sponge for stencilling 13 craft knife 14 craft knife blade and surgical blades

better to de-tack the tape slightly, which can be done by wiping each strip across lint-free cloth before use. De-tacked tape is sometimes available.

Matt emulsion, acrylic primer, undercoat, eggshell paint and varnishes

All of these are essentials. Manufacturers offer a huge range of options. Coverage and drying times vary, so follow the guidelines for individual products.

Matt emulsion glaze

This is a water-based medium used to thin colour and to act as a topcoat sealant for paint effects.

Measuring equipment

Use a tape measure for measuring and planning designs. A chalk line – a pin through a piece of string with chalk tied at one end – is useful for marking out large-scale images, geometric and circular shapes. A straight edge can be a long ruler or a piece of planed wood. A steel rule is preferable to plastic or wood as you will need a hard edge to ensure a straight, sharp cut when cutting stencils.

Metallic paints

Oil-based and acrylic paints are available in tubes and pots from good artist's suppliers and from some DIY shops. All vary in consistency. Another possibility is to mix your own, adding bronze powders to a diluted PVA base or button polish.

Paint-mixing containers

Use plastic paint kettles, clean jam jars, or any small containers such as clean yogurt and margarine pots, and tins. Use containers with tight-fitting lids for storing small amounts of paint: they should be labelled clearly. Always make

above: 1 dust sheet **2** stockinette cloth
3 surgical gloves **4** plastic sheeting
5 screwdriver **6** chalk and string with drawing pin **7** kitchen roll **8** pencil
9 mixing tray **10** decorator's sponge
11 cut sponge **12** jam jar
13 wet-and-dry sandpaper **14** filler knives **15** paint mixing containers and lids

1 chalk line, masking tape and wire wool
2 radiator roller with a short handle
3 wire brush, tape measure, steel rule and divider

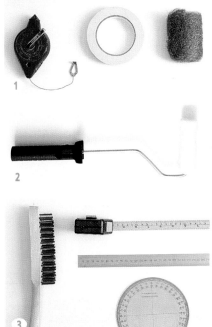

sure the container is durable if you are using it to store an unstable solution. Shallow containers can be used as mixing palettes.

Photocopier

A photocopier can be used to enlarge or repeat designs, to colour-copy items for découpage and to mock up ideas.

Protective clothing

Bib-and-brace overalls, thin surgical gloves, dust masks and goggles may all be needed. Any protective wear is recommended but it is important to choose things which allow freedom of movement. For example, if you choose to wear a hat or scarf, be careful that it does not impair your vision or balance, and if you are wearing boots make sure it is still possible to climb up and down a ladder without getting your feet caught.

Radiator roller and sponge roller heads

The size of this roller makes it especially useful for working on furniture and areas that are awkward to reach. The sponge heads are very handy for stencilling, giving an even paint coverage.

Sandpaper

You will need sandpaper in a selection of grades. Wet-and-dry paper is preferable for use on most painted surfaces. Although more expensive initially, it lasts longer and can be more easily controlled. Sanding blocks are not recommended as the resulting finish can be too flat.

Textured paints

Water-based paints such as masonry paint and matt emulsion can be used to create textured effects such as plaster by

the addition of sand and whiting or fillers used for fine filling.

Universal stainers, artist's oil and acrylic paints

Stainers can be added to any paint to add colour, but the choice is limited so often it is better to become familiar with the wide range of colours available from artist's and craft suppliers.

White spirit

Use to dilute oil-based paints for glazes and to clean brushes.

Wire wool and wire brush

These are mostly useful for keying surfaces to take paint. Wire wool can also be used to lightly remove a top coat and reveal areas of the base colour.

1 crackle-glaze **2** wax **3** PVA glue
4 matt emulsion **5** eggshell **6** matt emulsion glaze **7** acrylic metallic paint
8 metallic powders **9** powder pigment
10 artist's oil paint **11** watercolour
12 artist's acrylic paint **13** universal stainer **14** white spirit **15** oil varnish
16 Dutch metal leaf **17** gold size
18 metallic paint (on lid)

hints and tips

Stencil-cutting When cutting stencils, always score the surface slightly first, either with the drawing implement or a sharp point. This will give a depression for the knife to follow. Begin the cut at each corner or edge to lower the chances of overcutting the shape.

Colourwashing Always experiment with the dilute colour on a sample before beginning the project as colours vary greatly in consistency. Some have a higher quantity of pigment and the absorbency level of the surface will vary. Ensure the sample board has been prepared with the same base paint.

Mixing bronze powders Bronze powders come in many different colours and need a binder to make them workable. This can be PVA glue and a touch of water, sander/sealer or button polish (which gives a more luminous finish but dries very quickly), or wallpaper paste (this is a more transparent finish but less permanent, and needs to be well sealed with oil-based varnish). All colours will need sealing of some kind to reduce the chances of tarnishing. You will need to mix samples to obtain the depth of

colour required, and mix small amounts regularly while working. Avoid inhaling the powders when mixing and spoon out carefully.

Crackle-glaze – adding filler to emulsion top coat This method of crackle-glaze ensures a strong finish and gives the most authentic illusion of old worn paint, but it can result in quite a thick build-up of layers so will be unsuitable for some areas. It is not possible to suggest the exact proportions of filler to paint as products vary so greatly in consistency.

Care of brushes This is the most important job at the end of any project but often the most neglected. Brushes should be rinsed through with the appropriate thinner then washed out with washing-up liquid and water. Always store brushes carefully to avoid the bristles being bent. During use always stand brushes in water or thinner. Before using a new brush for the first time, rinse it through with washing-up liquid and water as this helps keep the bristles from shedding.

Ecology, spirits, storing paints Most of the projects in this book are achieved with the use of small amounts of water-soluble products. This demonstrates how much is possible with minimal impact on the environment. Where possible, keep mixed colours in recycled containers such as jam jars for use in the future, labelled to avoid confusion. Paint and varnish pots should be stored in a dry place, preferably with the lid tight and the pot upside-down to ensure that any skin forms at the bottom of the container. Used spirits can be poured into a container and re-used when the sediment has settled to the bottom or is sieved out.

If solvents and paints need to be disposed of, mark the containers and leave out for collection separately from general rubbish. Be aware that any cloths used with spirit-based products may combust if left in a warm environment.

Preparation of surfaces All the projects in the book include instructions for preparing the surface to emphasize the importance of this procedure. When working on walls which have been rollered with a base coat, stipple all corners and edges with the base colour rather than finishing with a brush stroke as the textural difference will show through most paint effects as a dark area. If you are working in dilute colour on walls or furniture it is important to keep the prepared surface as even as possible, as every mark will show through.

To prepare a sponge Most decorator's sponges come in a heat-sealed rectangular shape. The sponge is too big for most uses and the edges are too hard. Cut the sponge in half or quarters with a sharp knife and trim off the edges. The edges can be picked out more to imitate a natural sponge if you wish. The sponge should be washed in soapy water to remove any dye residue and rinsed in water. Sponges can be used for stencilling, texturing and colourwashing and will last better if they are always kept damp while in use. Clean the sponge in soapy water at the end of each day.

resources

painting supplies and decorating tools

J.W. Bollom
13 Theobald's Road
London WC1X 8FN
tel: 0171 2420313
Showroom
314-316 Old Brompton Road
London SW5 9JH

C. Brewers
327 Putney Bridge Road
London SW15 2PG
tel: 0181 7889335
branches throughout S.E. England

Brodie and Middleton Ltd
68 Drury Lane
London WC2B 5SP
tel: 0171 8363289

Cornelissen and Son Ltd
105 Great Russell Street
London WC1B 3RY
tel: 0171 6361045

Craig & Rose plc
172 Leith Walk
Edinburgh EH6 5EB
tel: 0131 5541131

Crown Berger Europe Ltd
P.O. Box 37
Crown House
Hollins Road
Darwen
Lancashire BB3 0BG
tel: 01254 704951

Dulux Decorating Centre
89 Richford Street
London W6 7HJ
tel: 0181 7490111

John T. Keep & Sons Ltd
15 Theobald's Road
London WC1X 8FN
tel: 0171 2427578

Keeps Ltd
PO Box 78
Croydon Road
Beckenham
Kent BR3 4BL
tel: 0181 6587723
glazes

Leyland SDM
The City
43–45 Farringdon Road
London EC1M
tel: 0171 242 5791

Milners
Canterbury Works
Cowley
Oxford OX4 2DP
tel: 01865 718171

Ray Munn
861-863 Fulham Road
London SW6 5HP
tel: 0171 7369876

The Paint Library
5 Elystan Street
London SW3 3NT
tel: 0171 8237755

The Paint Service Co. Ltd
19 Eccleston Street
London SW1 W9LX
tel: 0171 7306408

Paper and Paints
4 Park Walk
London SW10 0AD
tel: 0171 3528626

Potmolen Paint
27 Woodcock Industrial Estate
Warminster
Wiltshire BA12 9DX
tel: 01985 213960

J.H. Ratcliffe & Co. (Paints) Ltd
135a Linaker Street
Southport PR8 5DF
tel: 01704 537999

Simpsons Paints Ltd
122-124 Broadley Street
London NW8 8BB
tel: 0171 7236657

Unidec Distributors Ltd
165 Clapham High Street
London SW4 7SS
tel: 0171 7206746

artists' materials

Atlantis Art Materials
146 Brick Lane
London E1 6RU
tel: 0171 3778855
runs a mail order service

Daler-Rowney Ltd.
12 Percy Street
London W1A 2BP
tel: 0171 6368241

Green & Stone
259 King's Road
London
tel: 0171 3520837

W. Habberley Meadows Ltd
5 Saxon Way
Chelmsley Wood
Birmingham B37 5AY
tel: 0121 7702905

Lewis Ward & Co.
128 Fortune Green Road
London NW6 1DN
tel: 0171 7943130
specialist brushes

John Myland
80 Norwood High Street
London SE27 9NW
tel: 0181 6709161

E. Ploton (Sundries) Ltd
273 Archway Road
London N6 5AA
tel: 0181 3482838

Michael Putman
151 Lavender Hill
London SW11 5QJ
tel: 0171 2073055

Stuart R. Stevenson
68 Clerkenwell Road
London E3
tel: 0171 2531693
gilding materials

books

Dover Books
18 Earlham Street
London WC2H 9LN
tel: 0171 8362111
reference and stencil books

**interior design
and decoration**

BowWow
70 Princedale Road
London W11 4NL
tel: 0171 7928532

Creative Covers and Curtains
First Floor
61 Burton Road
Kingston Upon Thames
Surrey KT2 5TG
tel: 0181 5492054

The Carpet Library
148 Wandsworth Bridge Road
London SW6 2UH
tel: 0171 7363664
floor covering specialists

Sampson Sobiye
c/o Bow Wow
creative soft furnishings

Suasion
35 Riding House Street
London W1P 7PT
tel: 0171 5803763
fabric dyes

Whaleys (Bradford) Ltd.
Harris Court
Great Horton
Bradford
West Yorkshire BD7 4EQ
tel: 01274 576718
*fabrics for hand painting
& dying*

gardens

Dominic Capon
Unit 9 Imperial Studios
Imperial Road
London SW6 2AG
tel: 0171 7363060

Woodhams (Landscape) Ltd
McKay Trading Estate
300 Kensal Road
London W10 5BZ
tel: 0181 9649818

paper

Paperchase
Books Etc.
19 Whiteleys
Queensway
London W2 4UN
tel: 0171 8311151
stores nationwide

Falkiner Fine Papers
76 Southampton Row
London WC1B 4AR
tel: 0171 831 1151
runs a mail order service

index

Entries in *italics* indicate projects

Acetate, 102

Bronze powders, 140
Brushes, care of, 140
Burnished gold wall, 30-33

Canvas floor cloth, 52-55
Chest of drawers, 88-91
Colour, 10-11, 12-13, 14-15, 136, 137
  hue, 10
  intensity, 10-11
  monochromatic, 10
  neutrals, 10
  primary, 10, 11
  saturation, see intensity
  secondary, 10
  shades, 10
  spectrum, 10
  tertiary, 10
  tints, 10
  tones, 10
  value, 10
  wheel, 10
Colour combinations, see colour schemes
Colour schemes, 10-11, 14
Colourwash, 11, 12-13, 26, 30, 34-37, 58, 60, 62, 66, 68, 88, 140
Concrete, 124
Crackle-glaze, 12-13, 26-29, 84-87, 90-91, 137, 139, 140
Craquelure, see crackle-glaze

Dado, 66-69
Découpage leaf chest, 100-103
Découpage wall, 22-25
Disguised cupboards, 66-69
Distemper, 13
Dutch gold metal leaf, 68, 80-83, 139

Etching liquid, glass, 94-95

Fabrics, 104-117
Floors and floor coverings, 38-55
Furniture, painted, 74-103

Garden wall border, 132-135
Gardens, 118-139
Geometric floor border, 44-47
Geometric shapes, 44, 52
Gesso, 92, 94-95, 136
Gilded bedhead, 80-83
Gilding, 30, 80-83
Gold size, acrylic, 82-83

Handpainted curtains, 106-109
Harlequin cupboard, 76-79
Hints and tips, 140

Iridescent furniture, 120-123
Ironing, 108-109, 112-113

Light, 12
  halogen bulbs, 12
  natural light, 12
Lilac colourwash, 34-37
Lilac crackle-glaze panelling, 26-29
Limed effect floor, 40-43
Limewashing, 13, 40

Materials and equipment, 136-139
Matt emulsion glaze, 138
Measuring equipment, 138

Opalescence, 68, 92-95
Opalescent mirror frame, 92-95

Paint, 12-13, 136-137, 138-139
  fabric paints, 137
  medium, 13
  metallic paints, 12-13, 44, 46-47, 66, 67-69, 70-73, 78-79, 120-123, 138, 46-47, 76, 86-87

mixing containers, 138-139
  opalescent paints, 92-95
  pigment, 13, 20
  rollers, 139
  storing, 140
  textured paints, 139
  traditional paints, 13
Painted Roman blind, 110-113
Painted sisal rug, 48-51
Painted storage box, 96-99
Patio wall and arbour, 128-131
Pattern, 12, 14
Photocopying, 14, 102-103, 139
Plastering, 13, 18-21, 134-135
Polo lampshade, 114-117
Protective clothing, 139

Rothko kitchen units, 44, 70-73

Samples and ideas boards, 14-15
Sandpaper, 139
Sandstone fireplace, 62-65
Sandstone floor, 124-127
Special features, 56-73
Sponges, preparation of, 140
Stainers, 139
Stencilling, 32-33, 34-37, 46-47, 60-61, 78-79, 86-87, 90-91, 116-117, 134-135, 132-135, 136-137, 140
Stippling, 62, 65, 95
Striped door surround, 58-61
Stucco plaster effect, 18-21
Surface, preparation of, 140

Table-top border, 84-87
Texture, 10, 12, 14, 66, 136
Trompe l'oeil, 128
Tongue & groove panelling, see *lilac crackle-glaze panelling*

Walls, 16-38

acknowledgements

I would like to thank the following people for all their hard
work and help with the production of this book: Emily Truss,
Tabitha McBeth, Jeremy Underhill and Lee Quinn, my very
special assistants! Also to Cri Passmore, Geriant Williams
and, particularly, Naomi Hines.

David George and Tim French for their fab photographs.

Ahmed Sidki from BowWow for support and his team,
Alisdair, Sean, Mark and Matthew. And thanks to Rob, Eric,
Ian, Terry and Nicola for great work.

I am grateful to Steve White and Karen Colgnese for their trust
whilst watching their homes transformed! Francis Power for
hours of listening and proofing, thankyou! Particular thanks to
Tony, Clare and Goodfellow for CoCo care, and to my family
and Catherine Carnie for starting me off in a career I love.

Last but hardly least, Tessa Evelegh, Fiona Eaton and Ali Myer
for their confidence in the start and finish of the project.

For their generosity in supplying items for the photographs I
would like to thank:

Adam Aaronson (glass designer maker), Roxby Place, London
S6 1RS; Buyers and Sellers, 120-122 Ladbroke Grove, London
W105NE, tel: 0171 229 1947; The Cross, 141 Portland Road,
London W11, tel: 0171 727 6760; Rob Fawcett (specialist
design and metalwork), 44 Forest Lane, Stratford, London
E15 1HA; Clare Halvis (ceramic artist and maker), Studio W3
Cockpit Yard, London WC1N 2NF; Anthony Stern Glass,
Unit 205, Avro House, Havelock Terrace, London SW8 4AL.

Craig and Rose, Leyland SDM, Ray Munn, Unidec, Martin
Long of The Carpet Library, Whaleys (Bradford) Ltd,
Woodhams (Landscape) Ltd, Bow Wow, Babylon Design,
Emma Andrew, DWCD, Dominic Capon, Vikki Richards,
Clare Kalvis, Sampson and Peter Adler for his inspiring
collection.